RENEWING AMERICA'S CITIES

Thomas F. Johnson
James R. Morris
Joseph G. Butts

THE INSTITUTE FOR SOCIAL SCIENCE RESEARCH
Continental Building
Washington 5, D.C.
1962

© 1962 The Institute For Social Science Research. All rights reserved
under International and Pan-American Copyright Conventions
Library of Congress catalog card number: 62-12908

Printed in the United States of America
by
Graphic Arts Press, Washington, D.C.

Foreword

Recent debates in Congress on the President's proposal to create a Cabinet Department of Urban Affairs and Housing have focused public attention upon the problems involved in urban redevelopment. Although *Renewing America's Cities* does not deal with this proposal, as such, it presents a timely and informative study of the basic policies involved in current efforts to redevelop and rehabilitate cities and metropolitan areas.

The Federal Government became involved in slum clearance and the construction of low-rent public housing during the depression of the 1930's as a temporary unemployment relief measure. Federal participation has continued during the ensuing three decades and has expanded and developed into what is now known as "urban renewal."

The authors of *Renewing America's Cities* have placed the major problems of urban renewal in perspective by reviewing what has been, and is being, accomplished by governmental and private activities. The evolution of the role of the National Government in urban renewal activities is thoroughly traced, and urban renewal legislation and activities are discussed along with suggested guidelines for urban renewal programs. Included, also, is an analysis of the constitutional concepts involved in urban renewal.

The study is the work of two economists and an attorney. Dr. Thomas F. Johnson has had long experience in the field of public policy research. He was Assistant Commissioner of the Federal Housing Administration in charge of research and legislation from 1954 to 1958, during which time the urban renewal provisions of the National Housing Act of 1954 were being implemented. He has taught at the University of Virginia and George Washington University and is the author of numerous publications.

Dr. James R. Morris, a consulting economist, was for a number of years engaged in teaching and research at the Universities of Illinois, Chicago, and Arkansas. He is author of *Employment Opportunities in Later Years*, published by the Foundation for Voluntary Welfare, and articles in numerous professional journals.

Mr. Joseph G. Butts, a member of the District of Columbia Bar, was associated for some years with the Washington law firm of Gall, Lane and Howe. Formerly, he was Administrative Assistant to the late Representative John H. Kerr (N.C.). Mr. Butts has contributed numerous articles to legal journals and other publications.

The authors have had the benefit of comments and suggestions by many with extensive knowledge and experience in urban renewal activities; particularly, Mr. W. Beverley Mason, Jr., former Assistant Commissioner for Technical Standards of the Federal Housing Administration, and former Special Assistant for Urban Renewal in the office of the Commissioner of FHA. Mr. Mason worked closely with the authors in developing and drafting parts of the study.

The able assistance of Mrs. Betty Benswanger and Miss Frances McGavin in preparing the manuscript is gratefully acknowledged.

W. GLENN CAMPBELL
Chairman, Board of Trustees
The Institute for Social Science Research

Contents

CHAPTER I

The Urban Renewal Process

The Problem

AMERICA IS RAPIDLY becoming an urban nation—nearly 60 percent of our people live in the metropolitan areas.[1] Two-thirds of the increase in population between 1950 and 1959 occurred in these areas and the greater part of future population increases will be in the urban regions.

Sprawling urban or metropolitan growth has superseded city or town growth. Population is concentrating in great areas embracing multiple towns, cities, and suburbs. Moreover, concentration of population in metropolitan areas is being accompanied by sharp shifts of the population within these areas. Whereas population growth was once found in the cities, the suburbs now have the preponderant growth. Nearly the entire metropolitan growth between 1950 and 1959 was in the suburban population. Central city population actually declined between 1956 and 1959. Coupling these facts with the one that a substantial part of the central city population is becoming composed of lower income and minority groups helps bring some of the cities' problems into focus.

Almost every American city contains sizable blighted areas— residential, commercial, and industrial. Old, often overcrowded structures, generally located on outmoded street patterns, increase the costs of many municipal services, detract from the residential and commercial desirability of the areas and frequently contribute to a decreasing revenue base. Older residential areas that were once the better living areas in the city have deteriorated as higher income families have moved to newer locations. The passing of housing to occupancy by groups having lower living standards almost inevitably results in a decline in the quality of

---

[1] See Bureau of the Census definition of Metropolitan Area, p. 15, footnote 7.

the housing and this in turn accelerates the departure from the neighborhood of families with higher living standards.

This problem of older, degenerating urban areas is an old one; it has certainly been with us since the Industrial Revolution created rapid urbanization and will continue to be with us in the future. There is nothing new about blighted neighborhoods and slums in our cities—they are a result of growth and obsolescence and are intimately a part of the histories of cities.

Cities are the result of accumulation. Over a period of time, population and economic activities have become concentrated in certain areas. Such concentrations have arisen because within the areas of concentration certain advantages accrue to persons and organizations located there. These advantages are of various kinds such as terminal transportation facilities; proximity to resource and product markets, including highly specialized services; and ease of effective communication. Cities and their components are aggregations which have developed to perform given functions in answer to specific needs.

Various components of a city wear out or become obsolete in time. Street pavements gradually degenerate through heavy usage and as a result of weathering. Street and block layouts become ill-suited to changed uses and demands made upon them. Water and sewer systems eventually suffer from corrosion and disintegration. Industrial, commercial, residential, and governmental buildings and facilities gradually deteriorate from use and from the forces of nature. Cities typically do not arise as full-blown, fully-developed units. Because they are accretions of buildings, streets, public facilities, mass transit systems, and so on, which have accumulated over a period of time, parts of a city at any given time will be old and worn out.[2] Physical deprecia-

---

[2] Miles L. Colean very aptly illustrates this point in his study *Renewing Our Cities* (New York: The Twentieth Century Fund, 1953). He states: "A city in which there were not at all times some worn-out or obsolete parts would not be a dynamic city. The feature that gives restored Williamsburg its unreal quality is the good condition of all of it. No part is more obsolete than another. Nothing is on the way out; nothing new is pressing for its place on the Green. It is frozen in time, with no prospect of change." (p. 6)

tion begins as soon as a facility is constructed.

Growth as well as technological innovation renders portions and specific facilities inadequate. Technical developments made the gas street lamp obsolete and more recently even the familiar incandescent light bulb is being displaced. Mass transit systems and automobiles, in their turn, have worked enormous changes on and in the cities. The automobile has functioned as both cause and effect in influencing changes in street patterns, parking facilities, the flows of economic resources and economic products, and the location of dwellings and of production activities. Obsolescence is characteristic of a dynamic economy.

Within a city, resources will be used in different ways at different times. A church building may successively serve a church, an educational institution, and as a meeting hall before its demolition is warranted. A parcel of land may stand vacant, serving as an informal recreation area, becoming thereafter the site of a town house which in turn may give way to an apartment building, or even to a parking area. The residence of 50 years ago designed for a large family with one or more servants may stand vacant, the victim of a changing social order, until it becomes available for a rooming house. A river front, once the site of a fur trader's post, today may be the site of a restaurant specializing in sea foods, a national park, or an industrial plant. A modest row house of the 1920's is sold and resold, frequently each resale being to a member of a lower income group, thus satisfying the demand of those who cannot afford newly constructed housing. Resource use patterns constantly change in response to changes in demand and supply (cost) conditions. Resources are constantly in the process of being reallocated from one use to another.

The foregoing are the three basic factors which give rise to the problems of urban renewal: physical deterioration, obsolescence, and the reallocation of physical resources in response to economic and social pressures.

Physical deterioration requires a continuing program of maintenance if the structures and facilities of the city are not to become shabby and rundown. Streets and other public improvements must be mended and repaired periodically. Buildings,

[3]

whether residential, commercial, industrial, or governmental, require repairs, replacement of worn parts, painting, cleaning, and so on. In short, every individual component of the city must be given regular and effective maintenance.

Eventually, various units reach a stage at which further physical maintenance for their continued use is no longer economically feasible. Structures which have reached this stage should then be demolished. Thereafter, new uses of the site can follow. Some cleared sites may remain vacant for a period of time. Others may serve substantially the same purposes as before—a new house being erected on the cleared site of an old house. Still others may undergo a complete change in use such as occurs when a former residential area becomes commercial.

Thus the city has the twofold problem constantly confronting it: in the first instance, the problem of maintaining its parts or units in good condition and through exercise of police power to prevent abuses which are detrimental to whole neighborhoods; beyond this, it has the problem of seeing to it that those segments which can no longer be feasibly maintained and protected are eliminated. Failure to perform adequately and continuously these two functions results in the accumulation of wornout, unsightly, or even hazardous and unhealthy components of the city. If dilapidation or over-occupancy is permitted to continue, there is a tendency for it to spread its influence to widening perimeters, and blight and slums ensue. There is nothing mysterious about this; if a city is not to fall into decay, its individual components must be maintained, protected, and eventually replaced, if replacement is warranted. This is one aspect of urban renewal.

Structures and facilities not only wear out but they also become outmoded. Many of them outlive their usefulness. New needs and requirements may render them obsolete if they are not renovated and modernized in accord with prevailing standards and needs. An urban dwelling unit which lacks a flush toilet is an anachronism, from the standpoint of both current preferences and the sanitation requirements of a congested area. Failure to upgrade such a dwelling unit or to demolish it if upgrading is not feasible, will add to the backwash of blight and slum which can

[4]

infect the cities. New manufacturing techniques which require single-story rather than multi-story structures have rendered many industrial buildings obsolete for their original purposes. They must be converted to other uses or, alternatively, razed to make way for other uses of their sites. Failure to reutilize or to demolish outmoded factory buildings likewise may contribute to blighting of the city. Upgrading, use-conversion, and demolition are characteristic aspects of urban renewal which are essential derivatives of the obsolescence which results from technological innovation or from market changes.

A city is a dynamic and changing institution. Land-use patterns are constantly shifting in response to changes in demand and cost conditions. Space previously occupied by several small stores may be occupied by an office building. A higher use has supplanted a lower use; that is, as a result of change, it now is economically desirable for the office building, but uneconomic for the stores, to occupy that particular space. A group of houses may be demolished and a shopping center with parking space established on the sites which they once occupied. Changes of this type are a vital part of urban renewal. The reallocation of resources is necessarily a continuing process in any dynamic or changing situation.

Basic changes in our economy during the last few decades have contributed to a change in the role of the central cities as well as to changes in the internal conditions of the central cities. Private automobile transportation has made it possible for workers, no longer primarily dependent upon public transport, to live well outside the central parts of the cities. Motor truck transport has contributed to the declining relative importance of rail transport terminal facilities, thus contributing to the location of industry in what was once rural countryside. Technological changes in manufacturing have caused the multi-story factory to give way to the single-story building in some instances. Frequently, increased land requirements for single-story buildings make vacant land in the suburbs more attractive than more costly land in the central cities. Parking lot requirements for employees' automobiles also often encourage location in less congested areas.

[5]

The growth of suburban shopping centers has made it possible for many consumers to discontinue trading in the downtown commercial districts of the central cities. Observers point out that there has been a flight predominantly of the middle classes from the city to the suburbs. Recent metropolitan population growth has taken place primarily in the areas outside of the central cities. Also, the migration of minority groups into the central cities has contributed to housing and other internal problems of the cities.

The declining rate of growth in the central cities of itself can be a cause of anxiety to city officials if previous financing plans have been based upon the projection of a constant or even rising rate of growth. Added to this is the fact that the demand for services in the cities has not abated. Garbage still must be collected, fires fought, and police protection provided. Some observers have noted also that the various welfare services liberally extended by some cities function as magnets to attract great numbers of low-income persons and that this in turn magnifies the social and economic problems in the central cities. Factors such as the above have been discussed at length under such colorful titles as "The Plight of Our Cities" and "Are Our Cities Dying?"

Significantly, if the city has performed its housekeeping functions well—that is, if it has properly protected and maintained its structures and facilities during their economic life, upgraded or converted to other uses those structures and facilities whose upgrading or conversion is justified, and demolished those whose maintenance no longer is justified—the later phase of urban renewal—changes in the use of resources—will be greatly facilitated and generally will take place in response to market forces. To the extent that a city fails to perform adequately its functions of protection, maintenance, conservation, appropriate use conversion, and, where necessary, demolition and redevelopment, it fails to execute fundamental aspects of urban renewal, impedes enormously the changing of land-use patterns, and thus stagnates areas into blight and slum. Urban renewal is a process of city or urban self-regeneration and, as such, is dependent upon appropriate and continuing action to assure the regenerative process. It is a joint function of the individual property owners and their elected officials. Clearly, urban renewal in its broad sense is imperative to the preservation of the vitality of our cities. Yet within the last decade or so, urban renewal also has become something of a catch-phrase which is injected into most discussions of city problems. There has developed a federal grant-in-aid urban renewal program for aiding cities in undertaking broad redevelopment programs.

Rebuilding, rehabilitating, and renewing structures and changing land uses is a continuing process largely motivated by and in response to multitudinous private, market oriented decisions. In cities and urban areas these private decisions involving property and land uses are circumscribed by various legal restrictions whose objectives are mutual protection for the common good. These restrictions seek to insure minimum standards of safety and health and to prevent one or a few property or land owners from jeopardizing the use and enjoyment by others of their own properties.

Thus, zoning regulations aid in protecting and stabilizing property values by restricting non-harmonious uses within certain areas. Building and housing codes have similar purposes and effects. Such restrictions and requirements are necessary companions to private orderly development and use of urban land and structures. They serve as the means of assuring the maintenance of standards and use requirements which the community deems necessary for preventing rapid deterioration in property values and uses. As such, they can serve as a principal vehicle for encouraging and often enforcing a flexible, continuous urban renewal process. Many feel that this exercise of certain police powers by local government is as far as public action should go.

On the other hand, some say we must completely renew, rebuild, and rearrange the older sections of our cities, though the cost may be great and though public subsidy may be necessary. This approach to urban renewal raises interesting questions.

There is little doubt that we have sufficient total economic resources to rebuild and modernize all such areas within our cities if we wish to do so and to forego the fruits of alternative uses of the resources so committed. But the fact that substantial public subsidy for property accumulation and write-down of land value is required to make many such projects feasible, raises questions concerning the efficient use of economic resources.

Such a program might be compared, by way of hypothetical example, to one for producing all of our coffee in the United States. Technologically no great problems exist and we certainly have the resources if we wish to so use them. But does such a use of resources make economic sense? Without large public subsidy, coffee would become a high-priced luxury item. And with a subsidy, the cost to consumers as a group (taxpayers) would still be much more than at present. Similarly, clearing deteriorating structures from large areas in our cities and redeveloping and rebuilding these areas with modern facilities and structures, often of luxury types, frequently involves large public cost (subsidy). Most certainly the areas involved will be upgraded and improved in value. But does such a program represent an efficient use of resources? The fact that substantial subsidy is involved raises serious doubt. Is the net gain from the subsidy dollar, spent to make the particular project possible, equal to or greater than the gain from the use of the same dollar elsewhere?

Here, then, are two different (but not mutually exclusive) approaches. They both have been used and are being used in various combinations. Some of the problems and results are examined in the subsequent pages.

[8]

CHAPTER II

Housing and Urban Renewal

HOUSING IS ONE of the most important components of national wealth. It is also a most important element in urban renewal programs and the major focus of federal urban renewal legislation. Examination of some of the quantitative and qualitative changes in the housing inventory of the country, therefore, is necessary in order to gain some perspective of the urban renewal problem—especially as it pertains to housing.

Americans have been improving their housing steadily over the last half century, and at a particularly rapid pace since World War II. Today the great majority of American housing meets the tests of quality for standard housing—it is adequate and safe structurally, and has essential facilities such as private toilets, bath, and hot and cold running water. Substandard housing, which lacks one or more of these, is most numerous outside metropolitan areas (particularly in rural areas) and in the older sections of cities. While the greater portion of such housing is outside the metropolitan areas, urban renewal programs are primarily focused upon the cities.

A look at some of the census data on housing reveals the vast improvement and substantial increase in the housing stock that have occurred in the postwar years.[1] In 1950, 63 percent of the housing units on which the census data indicated condition, were of standard quality. In 1960, over 80 percent of total units were so classified.[2] Furthermore, dilapidated units as defined by the

---

[1] The 1960 Census of Housing is the third such decennial census in the United States, although a special survey of the housing inventory was made by the Census Bureau in 1956 and some housing data were collected in earlier years in connection with other censuses.

[2] Units including all facilities and not dilapidated. The 1960 Census data included the category of "Deteriorating" which indicated substantial repair was needed if the unit was to continue to provide adequate shelter. Those units in this category with all facilities were included in the above percentage.

Bureau of the Census[3] have not only declined percentage-wise in relation to the total stock, but have been reduced in actual numbers (Table I).

Table I
Housing Units by Condition 1950, 1956, and 1960

	1950	1956	1960
	thousands		
Total	45,983	55,342	58,324
Units reporting condition	44,502	53,381	------
Standard[1]	28,102	40,753	47,372
Dilapidated	4,339	4,055	3,025

[1] Includes units that are not dilapidated and contain private toilet and bath, and hot running water.

Source: U.S. Bureau of the Census, *Census of Housing: 1950*, Vol. I, Part 1, Table 7, p. 1–4; U.S. Bureau of the Census, *1956 National Housing Inventory*, Vol. III, Part 1, Table 1, p. 16; U.S. Bureau of the Census, *Census of Housing: 1960*, Advance Reports, HC(A1)–52, Table 1, p. 5.

The tremendous volume of new residential construction since World War II has been the major factor in improving the quality of American housing. However, upgrading of existing units is also an important factor in the overall improvement of the housing inventory. Some 3.4 million units were upgraded to standard condition (not dilapidated, with all facilities), in the 1950-1956 period. There was some downgrading as well: 1.3 million units were downgraded from standard quality to lacking facilities or dilapidated.[4] This represented a substantial net gain in quality for the Nation's housing inventory, a net of 2.1 million units were upgraded to standard quality. Two-thirds of these 2.1 million units were outside metropolitan areas, and 13.5 percent were in the older central city areas.[5]

---

[3] The 1960 Census of Housing defined dilapidated housing as that which "does not provide safe and adequate shelter. It has one or more critical defects; or has a combination of intermediate defects; or is of inadequate original construction. Critical defects are those which indicate continued neglect and serious damage to the structure."

[4] U. S. Bureau of the Census, *1956 National Housing Inventory*, Vol. I, Part 1, Table 4, p. 35.

[5] *Ibid.*

Housing Quality

Over three-fourths of the nearly 50 million *occupied* dwelling units in 1956 were of standard quality and contained all facilities. The largest percentages of dilapidated housing were outside the standard metropolitan areas (SMA), and in the central cities within such areas. (Table II) The lowest percentages of standard housing were in these areas. The parts of the standard metropolitan areas outside the central cities (usually the rapidly growing suburbs) had the highest percentage of standard quality housing (86.7 percent) and the lowest percentage of dilapidated housing (3.1 percent). Also, renter-occupied housing had a lower percentage of standard units than did owner-occupied housing.

The standard metropolitan areas, which contained about 60 percent of all occupied units, had only a little more than one-third of the dilapidated units. Areas outside the SMAs, with about 40 percent of the occupied units, had nearly two-thirds of the dilapidated dwellings. Rural farm and non-farm housing contained the largest number of substandard and dilapidated units—the 1950 housing census attributed 58 percent of the dilapidated units to rural housing. Within the SMAs, the central cities and the areas outside these cities contained close to the same number of occupied units, but the central cities had 50 percent more dilapidated units than the surrounding areas outside the central cities. The problem of upgrading housing then is concentrated largely in the older section of central cities and rural areas.

Population and Housing

The number of housing units has grown more rapidly than has population—this is true for occupied housing units as well as for the housing inventory as a whole. While the "population explosion" has received much attention, we also have experienced what might be called a "housing explosion." Nearly seven-eights as many non-farm housing units were built from 1950 through 1960 as in the preceding 30 years, including the housing boom of the

Table II
Occupied Dwelling Units[1] by Location, Tenure, and Condition, 1956

	Total (millions)	Total (percent)	Standard[2] (millions)	Standard[2] (percent)	Dilapidated[3] (millions)	Dilapidated[3] (percent)
All Occupied Units	49,874	100	38,119	76.4	3,027	6.3
Owner occupied	30,121	100	24,487	81.3	1,072	3.6
Renter occupied	19,753	100	13,632	69.0	1,955	9.9
Inside SMAs,[4] total	29,778	100	25,626	86.1	1,111	3.7
Owner occupied	17,275	100	15,733	91.1	321	1.9
Renter occupied	12,503	100	9,893	79.1	790	6.3
Inside SMAs in Central Cities	15,507	100	13,257	85.5	669	4.3
Owner occupied	7,041	100	6,565	93.2	98	1.4
Renter occupied	8,466	100	6,692	79.0	571	6.8
Inside SMAs not in Central Cities	14,271	100	12,369	86.7	442	3.1
Owner occupied	10,234	100	9,168	89.6	223	2.2
Renter occupied	4,037	100	3,201	79.3	219	5.4
Outside SMAs	20,096	100	12,493	62.2	1,915	9.5
Owner occupied	12,845	100	8,754	68.2	751	5.8
Renter occupied	7,251	100	3,739	51.6	1,164	16.1

[1] Generally, a dwelling unit is a house, an apartment or a flat. Trailers, boats, tents, and railroad cars, when occupied as living quarters, are included in the dwelling unit inventory; if vacant, such accommodations are excluded.
[2] Standard units are not dilapidated and contain all plumbing facilities (private toilet and bath and hot running water).
[3] Dilapidated units were in such condition as not to provide adequate shelter or protection against the elements or endangered the safety of the occupants. The condition could be due to deterioration or inadequate original construction.
[4] Standard Metropolitan Area, except in New England, is defined as a county or group of contiguous counties which contained at least one city of 50,000 or more inhabitants at the time of the 1950 census.
Source: Computed from data in U.S! Bureau of the Census, *1956 National Housing Inventory*, Vol. III, Part 1, Table 8, pp. 32–34.

1920's.[5] Almost three-fourths of all these units built since 1950 have been located in the metropolitan areas.

A *net* of 12.2 million housing units (26.4 percent) were added to the housing inventory between 1950 and 1960. During the preceding decade of the 1940's, there was an 8.7 million *net* increase (23.2 percent). Thus, of the 58.3 million housing units recorded in the 1960 census, over 20 million or 36 percent were *net* additions in the preceding 20 years. Population rose 17.5 percent between 1950 and 1960 and 14.6 percent between 1940 and 1950 (Table III).

Table III
Increase in Housing Units[a] and Population, 1940 to 1960

Year	Housing Units			Population		
	Total	Increase	Percent	Total	Increase	Percent
	——millions——		Increase	——millions——		Increase
1940	37.3	----	----	132.0	----	----
1950	46.1	8.7	23.2	151.3	19.3	14.6
1960	58.3	12.2	26.4	177.9	26.6	17.5

[a] In the 1960 census, the term housing unit was substituted for dwelling unit and some changes in definition were made as well. The newer term of housing units which in brief may be regarded as private or separate living quarters used here. Although the definitional changes will make some difference in the housing statistics they are sufficiently comparable for general purposes. The 1960 census includes all private living accommodations—a more inclusive concept than that used in earlier censuses. A housing unit is separate if its occupants do not live and eat with another household and if there is direct access from outside or through a common hall, or if the unit has its own cooking facilities for its occupants' exclusive use. The Census Bureau estimated that the new definition would add about one million units—two percent—to the total housing inventory. These additional units generally would be rooms in converted structures, rooming houses, and non-transient hotels. (See press release from U.S. Department of Commerce, titled *1960 Housing Census Includes New Subjects*, release date of February 28, 1960, p. 102).

Source: U.S. Bureau of the Census, *Census of Housing: 1950*, Vol. I, Part 1, Table G, p. XXVII; U.S. Bureau of the Census, *Census of Housing: 1960*, Preliminary Reports, Housing Unit Counts, HC(P1)–1, September 1960, p. 1; U.S. Bureau of the Census, *United States Census of Population: 1960*, Preliminary Reports, Population Summaries, PC(P3)–4, October 1960, Table A; U.S. Bureau of the Census, *Statistical Abstract of the United States: 1959*, Table 2, p. 5.

[5] **New Nonfarm Dwelling Units Started by Decades, 1910-1960**

Year	Number of Units (thousands)
1910–1919	3,593
1920–1929	7,034
1930–1939	2,734
1940–1949	5,683
1950–1960	13,441

Source: U.S. Bureau of the Census, *Statistical Abstract of the United States: 1949, 1952, 1958, 1960, Economic Indicators*, Report of the Council of Economic Advisers, July 1961.

But, of greater significance is the growth in the number of *occupied* housing units relative to population. Data relative to occupied housing units give a better indication of how the population actually lives than do the more inclusive figures for the total housing inventory. Since 1890, the growth of the occupied housing inventory has outstripped population growth, reflecting the long-term tendency towards smaller household units and smaller families. In the 70-year period 1890-1960, population increased by 183 percent while the number of occupied housing units increased by 318 percent. A steady decline in population per occupied housing unit has resulted. For the Nation as a whole, population per occupied housing unit declined from 4.3 in 1920 to 2.9 in 1960.[6]

Decline in household size reflects the decline in the birth rate in the 1930's which continued until the postwar population boom. Additionally the trend towards urbanization has been accompanied by a decline in the "three-generation" household. Increasingly, adults of all ages, single and married, tend to maintain their own households, living in separate housing units. Growth of the housing inventory more rapidly than population, reflects the high rate of household formation and the adaptability of the housing market to changing demands.

The long-term decline in the size of the average household has been accompanied by a tendency towards the construction of housing units of medium size. Whereas four-room and five-room units constituted 38.5 percent of the housing units in 1940, these sized units comprised 46.9 percent of housing units in 1956. Units containing one, two and three, and eight or more rooms suffered the largest relative declines. This substantial increase in the relative importance of moderate-sized housing units in the housing inventory again reflects the adaptability of the housing stock to changing demands by households and families. A smaller proportion of households now demand either the very small or the very large housing unit.

---

[6] U. S. Bureau of the Census, *Census of Housing: 1950,* Vol. I, Part 1; U. S. Bureau of the Census, *Census of Housing: 1960,* Advance Reports.

Table IV

Distribution of Rooms per Housing Unit

	1956	1950	1940
	percent		
1 room	2.2	2.9	3.5
2 and 3 rooms	18.5	22.4	23.2
4 and 5 rooms	46.9	43.1	38.5
6 and 7 rooms	26.0	24.2	25.0
8 rooms or more	6.4	7.4	9.8
	100.0	100.0	100.0

Source: U.S. Bureau of the Census, *U.S. Census of Housing: 1950*, Vol. I, Part 1, Table M; U.S. Bureau of the Census, *Statistical Abstract of the United States: 1959*, Table No. 1034.

Standard Metropolitan Areas[7]

Housing and construction follow people. Thus, as one would expect, the greatest growth of both population and housing has been in the suburban areas. A large percentage of older housing is, therefore, in the central portions of the cities—where population growth has been least rapid.

The phenomenal urbanization of the Nation was evident as a trend by 1930. Central city growth was reaching a peak while suburban growth awaited the impetus of the postwar expansion. The vast population shifts were accompanied by major readjustments in the housing market.

As indicated in Table V, the greatest population increases during the decades 1940-1950 and 1950-1960 occurred within standard metropolitan areas. Population rose 50 percent faster in these

[7] A standard metropolitan statistical area is defined by the Bureau of the Census as a county or group of contiguous counties which contain at least one city of 50,000 or more, (except in New England, where towns and cities are the units used in defining the areas). Counties contiguous to the county containing the central city are included if they are essentially metropolitan in character and are economically and socially integrated with the central city. Central cities are the major cities inside standard metropolitan statistical areas. This is a shortened, hence rough, statement of the detailed definition of standard metropolitan statistical areas. For the detailed definition, see *Census of Housing: 1950, op. cit.* (The term "standard metropolitan statistical areas" has replaced the term "standard metropolitan areas." The changed designation has *not* involved a change in definition.)

areas than for the country as a whole. Significantly, moreover, within the metropolitan areas population increases were much larger in the areas outside the central cities. These largely sub-urban areas had a population increase, between 1940 and 1950, two-and-a-half times that of the older central city areas, and between 1950 and 1960, an increase five times as great. The rate of population increase actually has been declining in the central cities.

Table V
Percentage Increases in Population and Housing
Standard Metropolitan Areas

	Population		Housing Units	
	1940–1950	1950–1960	1940–1950	1950–1956
	percent			
United States	14.5	17.5	23.2	20.3
Inside SMAs	22.0	25.3	28.3	23.4
In Central Cities	13.9	9.4	19.0	7.7
Outside Central Cities	35.6	47.7	44.4	45.9
Outside SMAs	6.1	6.5	17.3	16.6

Source: U.S. Bureau of the Census, *1950 Census of Population*, Advance Reports, Series PC–9, No. 6, November 24, 1952, p. 1; U.S. Bureau of the Census, *1960 Census of Population*, Preliminary Reports, Population Summaries, PC(P3)–4, October 1960, Table A; U.S. Bureau of the Census, *Census of Housing: 1950*, Vol. I, Part 1, Table G, p. XXVII; U.S. Bureau of the Census, *1956 National Housing Inventory*, Vol. I, Part 1, Table C, p. 15.

Increases in housing units followed the same pattern. Growth in units in metropolitan areas has outstripped that for the country as a whole. Within the metropolitan areas, the growth in the surrounding areas outside the central cities was over twice as great between 1940 and 1950 and over six times as great between 1950 and 1956.

The greater relative growth in the number of housing units in the standard metropolitan statistical areas outside of the central cities is a response to population shifts. The 1950's were a decade of suburbia. Not only has the population generally tended to concentrate in metropolitan areas, but also there has been a decreased tendency to live in the central cities. Preliminary reports from the Bureau of the Census have indicated a net population loss for some central cities, while many have experienced only slight population increases in the past decade. The declining relative importance of the central cities, from the standpoint of resident population, is emphasized by the low, and declining, rate of housing unit growth within central cities.

Age of the Housing Inventory

The average age of the stock of housing has been reduced significantly since the war, and particularly during the 1950's. In 1950, nearly eight out of ten houses had been built prior to 1940; by 1956, this had declined to a little over six in ten. Nearly all of the new building occurred outside the older central cores of the cities with the result that the older, less desirable, and often substandard non-farm housing units tended to be concentrated within the cores of the cities. This in itself is a major factor highlighting the demand for urban renewal by cities and focusing attention on the areas of greatest need.

The age of housing units helps to give some perspective of the housing market, although age itself is an inadequate criterion of housing conditions. For example, a century-old house may provide excellent housing while one 20 years old may expose its occupants to the elements or be a fire trap or other hazard to the safety of its inhabitants. The condition of housing depends primarily upon the nature of the original structure (materials and construction) and upon the maintenance and improvements it has received over time. Some 50-year-old housing units provide more satisfactory shelter and greater convenience than do some far newer dwelling units.

Probably no one really knows how long housing units will last. With appropriate care and maintenance, there is no precise limit to the economic life of a dwelling unit. Even rather inexpensive houses and apartments, if given proper maintenance will last many decades, providing good shelter for their inhabitants. There are many charming homes, a hundred or more years old in our country and considerably older in nations abroad, that are still serving as excellent shelter as well as meeting the other needs and desires of modern families. A dwelling is unlike any other consumer durable commodity in that it is usually easier and cheaper to upgrade, change, and modernize a house than to discard and renew it. It has been stated that a family can wear out almost any other possession during the lifetime of an individual, but it cannot wear out a home. A major contributing cause to the downgrading and obsolescence of housing and the creation of blighted areas is changes in neighborhood and other off-site conditions which detract from the desirability of the dwelling as a home and cause its owner to lose interest in maintaining it.

Both because of the aggregate expenditure required for a dwelling unit and because of its durability, the average age of our housing inventory at any given time will be substantial. New production runs around 3 percent annually. We consume a housing unit over a period of years, deriving a continuing stream of services and benefits from it, until finally we conclude that its continued maintenance is too costly relative to the satisfaction we derive from it. At this point it is ready usually for demolition.

In 1940, 41 percent of the Nation's housing units were in structures more than 30 years old.[8] Only 16 percent were less than ten years old. By 1950, 21 percent of the housing units were less than ten years old, reflecting the effects of the postwar building boom. However, retention of older structures led to an increase in the percentage of units over 30 years of age: from 41 percent in 1940 to 46 percent in 1950. This is closely akin to what happened in the postwar period with respect to the automobile inventory. The boom in automobile production in the postwar years put a large percentage of relatively new cars into the national automobile inventory. At the same time, retention of prewar cars led to an unusually large proportion of aged automobiles in the national inventory.

Between 1950 and 1956, some 10.9 million housing units were added to the national housing inventory through new construction.[9] These 10.9 million units (built 1950-56) constituted, in 1956, 20 percent of the 54.9 million housing units the age of which was reported in the 1956 inventory.

---

[8] *Census of Housing: 1950, op. cit.*, Vol. I, Part 1, Table N.
[9] *1956 National Housing Inventory*, Vol. I, Part 1, *op. cit.*, Table 1.

Viewing the housing inventory slightly differently, in 1950, 66 percent of the reported (as to age) housing inventory had been built before 1930 and 79 percent before 1940. Only six years later, in 1956, only 54 percent had been built before 1930 and 63 percent before 1940.[10]

These national figures obscure the fact that the age of housing units varies from area to area, reflecting in good part population growth and location. Thus, some towns and small cities are wholly new creatures of large-scale developers. The housing units in such areas may be all, or nearly all, new. Enormous growth in some suburban areas within standard metropolitan statistical areas has reduced the average age of housing units within these areas. In some central cities, however, particularly those of the East, new construction within the city proper has been relatively slight because of limited available land within the city limits, or because of the preference of builders and residents for sites in the suburban fringe areas, or because city limits could not be expanded as easily as they once were.

In any event, the continuing process of adding to the housing inventory has been by-passing many of the largest central cities in favor of development elsewhere. Thus, of the 10.9 million new units added through new construction between 1950 and 1956, 6.8 million units (62.4 percent) were within standard metropolitan areas.[11] However, only 1.8 million units (16.5 percent) were within the central cities.

The central cities reported (in 1956) by far the largest percentage of housing units built prior to 1930—69 percent. (Table VI) On the other hand, the suburban fringe, inside the standard metropolitan statistical areas but outside the central cities, had the smallest proportion of housing units built prior to 1930—37 percent. These latter areas are the areas of greatest population growth since World War II. Central cities, already heavily built-up and with relatively little vacant land, have been by-passed

---

[10] U. S. Bureau of the Census, *1956 National Housing Inventory,* Vol. III, Part 1, Table 1; *Census of Housing: 1950, op. cit.,* Table 6.

[11] *1956 National Housing Inventory,* Vol. I, Part 1, *op. cit.,* Table 1.

Table VI

Distribution of Dwelling Units Reported Built in 1929 or Earlier, as of December 1956

	Percent by area built in 1929 or earlier
All Dwelling Units-United States	54.0
Inside SMAs:	53.6
In Central Cities	68.8
Outside Central Cities	37.4
Outside SMAs	54.6

Source: Computed from U.S. Bureau of the Census, *1956 National Housing Inventory*, Vol. III, Part 1, Table 1.

for the most part by the housing boom as well as by the heavy population growth.

A casual glance at housing data for urbanized areas reveals the main force affecting age of dwelling units in various areas. Thus, in 1950, it was evident that the areas of great growth were the areas where the larger proportions of new housing units were located. Contrariwise, older areas of relatively little growth had the smaller proportions of new housing. Forty-seven percent of Miami, Florida's housing units (as of 1950) were in structures built in 1940 or later.[12] Fifty-one percent of those in Phoenix, Arizona were in this category. On the other hand, only 5 percent of New Bedford, Massachusetts' housing units had been built in 1950 or later. And only 0.9 percent of Scranton, Pennsylvania's housing units were in structures built in 1940 or later. The same kind of age distribution characterized the major regions of the Nation. The South and West, fast-growing regions, had substantially larger proportions of housing units in structures of recent vintage than did the older Northeast and North Central regions.[13]

Our oldest average age of housing tends to be in those areas where population and economic growth rates are lower than elsewhere. Population and economic activity are constantly changing their geographic location. Hence, it is neither surprising nor even deplorable that the age of dwelling units varies substantially

[12] *Census of Housing: 1950*, Vol. I, Part 1, *op. cit.*, Table 32.
[13] *Ibid.*

in different regions. This is to be expected in a dynamic society. These changes, however, do underscore the fact that as housing units age there exists the substantial problem of making sure that they age decently, if not gracefully. An isolated farm house in dilapidated condition is of little moment to anyone other than its occupants, but in the closely compressed central city, a dilapidated house or apartment building may begin the spread of blight and slums in the vicinity.

CHAPTER III

The Developing Federal Role

THE FEDERAL URBAN RENEWAL PROGRAM

THE FEDERAL URBAN renewal program had its genesis during the depression of the 1930's. President Hoover, toward the end of his term of office, convened a conference on rehabilitation and slum prevention. Federal loans were authorized and a number of recommendations based on the economic aspects of the problem evolved. However, the first direct action appeared during the depression of the 1930's, when the Federal Government embarked upon a number of projects designed to promote economic recovery, including highway construction, the erection of public buildings, slum clearance, and the provision of low-rent public housing. It was the program comprising slum clearance and public housing from which the present urban renewal program developed. The term "urban renewal" itself is of more recent vintage and has come to include many highly varied objectives in addition to slum clearance and housing, although these still appear at the heart of federal urban renewal activities.

As the need for contra-cyclical spending subsided, the program was expanded to carry out a more elaborate set of objectives. These objectives involve a variety of economic, sociological, welfare, and aesthetic considerations. Thus the program embraces, among other things, the concept of providing so-called "low-cost," or "low-rent" housing in order to assure adequate housing conditions for low-income groups. The term "low-cost housing" has caused considerable confusion. Actually, it is housing which in many instances is quite costly, but which is provided, by means of national government subsidy, to selected tenants at below market rents.

Aside from the confusion resulting from semantics, another element of confusion in urban renewal activities has arisen precisely because of the introduction of government subsidies. The subsidization by government of housing units built and maintained for and made available to selected groups of low-income persons has tended to confuse or to jumble together two entirely separate problems; namely, the problem of providing housing facilities and the problem of income distribution. As a result, some of those interested in urban renewal activities may be primarily concerned with redistributing income while others may be concerned with housing as such.

Sociologists and welfare workers have been keenly aware of the relationship between slums and antisocial behavior on the part of slum inhabitants. Imposing statistical data have been arrayed which show a disporportionate incidence of anti-social behavior among the inhabitants of slums. Frequently it has been said that slums, which often contain much substandard housing, are the breeding grounds of crime and vice. Hence, some welfare workers and others have urged that if slum dwellings were razed and their inhabitants rehoused in good, modern quarters, antisocial behavior might be checked. It has been urged that the change in environment, from substandard to standard housing facilities, would operate as a strong social reform force.[1] Thus, housing to promote social reform is considered by some as an important part of federally aided urban renewal.

Slums generally are characterized by overcrowding, inadequate santitation facilities and services, dilapidation of buildings, general unsightliness, and a disproportionate share of antisocial behavior among their inhabitants. Because of the reform motives previously mentioned, as well as the generally acknowledged undesirability of slums, the clearance of slums is one of the objectives of the federal urban renewal program.

Beyond these various goals, urban renewal is regarded by some as a means of creating what is sometimes characterized as "the

---

[1] There is considerable evidence to the contrary on this point. In some cases, public housing projects have been plagued with crime, juvenile delinquency, vandalism, and tenant damages and tenants have objected to changing their "antisocial" habits. See "Taxpayers Tenants," *The Wall Street Journal*, April 10, 1958; *Juvenile Delinquency*, Interim Report of the Committee on the Judiciary, U.S. Senate, March 1954, pp. 55-56; also "Our Antiseptic Slums," *The Newark Star-Ledger*, February 2, 1955.

city beautiful." Our cities long have been indicted by many observers as unplanned and haphazard in their growth, and as ugly and unattractive to the eye. Many persons view the urban renewal program as an opportunity to remake our cities into clean, well-planned, and aesthetically appealing places to work, live, and play. Supporters of this type of program generally picture a renewed city of broad boulevards, artistically landscaped parks, modern new structures, free-flowing traffic, and families who occupy charming garden apartments. Creating beautiful cities has become for many an important objective of urban renewal.

Intimately related to the desire to make our cities more beautiful is the objective of revivifying or revitalizing the cities. The Nation's population increasingly has been concentrated in urban areas, so that now about two-thirds of the population reside in such areas. The recent great population increases in the standard metropolitan areas have occurred for the most part, however, on the peripheries of the central cities. Indeed, while most central cities have not grown as rapidly as their satellite suburbs, some central cities have sustained absolute net population declines in recent years. The lower or even negative population growth of central cities has occasioned much concern among some observers of the urban scene. Some hold that the federal urban renewal program provides, or can provide, the basis for checking the declining relative importance of central cities as places in which to live. Some commentators believe that slum clearance, rebuilding, and beautification of the city with federal aid will serve to attract back into the central cities many of those who have moved to the suburbs. Urban renewal, hence, is viewed by some as a means of re-establishing the role of predominance which the central cities once occupied.

Finally, some persons view the federal program as a way of effecting a change in land-use patterns. For many of those who have a professional or political interest in urban renewal programs, there generally is an overlapping of the concept of changing land-use patterns with other objectives such as slum clearance, public housing, and beautifying and revitalizing the city. Thus, for example, slum clearance and the erection of high-rise apartment buildings on the former slum site is frequently cited as a "higher use" as a result of the urban renewal program. Or, as another example, the razing and bulldozing of an area of mixed residential and commercial buildings, followed by the construction of public housing units is regarded by some as an instance of achieving a higher land use.

In summary, the origin of federal urban renewal activities can be traced to the contra-cyclical expenditures program for slum clearance and public housing units during the depression of the 1930's. Subsequently, the contra-cyclical objective was abandoned. The slum clearance and housing objectives were retained and expanded, and a variety of other objectives were added as the program developed. The federal urban renewal program is variously regarded as a means of adding to, improving and conserving the national housing inventory, of redistributing income (providing subsidized low-rent housing), aiding in reforming antisocial behavior of slum inhabitants, making cities more beautiful places in which to live, work, and play, revitalizing cities whose relative importance has declined, and, finally, of bringing about changes in the land-use patterns within cities.

EVOLUTION OF URBAN RENEWAL LEGISLATION

State Legislation

State "Police Powers" and the "Nuisance Doctrine." Every state in the Union has the legal power to require the owners of slum properties to put them in decent condition or to demolish them. State laws for this purpose have grown out of what is known as the common law "doctrine of nuisances." The power to abate nuisances is derived from the basic general power of the states to regulate their internal affairs. The "nuisance doctrine" was a part of the common law of England. It evolved from the ancient and familiar legal maxim: "So use your own property as not to unreasonably injure others."[2] According to Blackstone, the nuisance doctrine of his day could be invoked to prevent "the doing of a thing to the annoyance of the King's subjects or the

---

[2] *Sic utere tuo ut alienum non laedas.* 39 *Am. Jur.* § 16.

neglecting to do a thing which the common good requires." The police power, including the power to abate nuisances, was vested in the states before the Constitution was adopted and reserved to them by the Tenth Amendment.[3] Broadly speaking, our state courts define a public nuisance as a condition which adversely affects the safety, health, or morals of the public.

A basic difference between the common law against nuisances and a modern housing code is that the former consists of a broad and somewhat flexible doctrine whereas the latter is contained in statutes, or ordinances, and spells out definitive housing standards. The common law doctrine is applied *de novo* by the local courts. Housing codes are enforced by administrative agencies subject to judicial review.

Housing (Anti-Slum) Codes. It has been said that local housing codes date back to Hammurabi who ruled the City of Babylon 2,000 years before Christ. Also, there were the ancient codes of the Chinese, Greeks, and Romans and the sanitary and safety requirements imposed in London in the 12th century, and after the fire of 1666.[4] In this country, Massachusetts enacted laws to control "nuisances affecting health and comfort" as early as 1692. A similar law was adopted by South Carolina at about the same time and by the City of Philadelphia in 1712.[5] By 1801, New York had provided for the inspection of buildings and had authorized Health Commissioners to deal with slum properties.[6]

A basic pattern of invoking state powers to eliminate slum properties in the interest of public health had become well established by 1893. A New York State law, in effect at that time, authorized Health Boards to "order the suppression and removal of nuisances and conditions detrimental to life and health." Such Boards were

---

[3] 11 Am. Jur. Constitutional Law § 247 (1937). "The police power is as old as the civilized governments which exercise it." *Id.*, § 245.

[4] "Housing Codes in Urban Renewal," paper presented at the annual meeting of the American Bar Association in 1956 by Joseph Guandolo, then Associate General Counsel, Urban Renewal Administration.

[5] *Ibid.*

[6] *Law and Contemporary Problems* (Durham, N. C.: Duke University School of Law, Winter 1947), p. 112.

directed to investigate complaints against slum properties and were given the power to inspect any premises where such conditions were believed to exist. Violations of Health Board orders or regulations were punishable as misdemeanors.[7]

The early New York law gave broad authority to administrative officials, but the rights of individual property owners were protected by the courts which held that those who administered the Act could not "make a nuisance which is not in fact a nuisance."[8]

Aside from the basic general police power to deal with slum conditions which constitute a "public nuisance," the President's Advisory Committee on Housing reported in 1953 that definitive "building, fire, housing, and health codes exist in nearly all cities."[9] This is not to say that all such codes are as comprehensive as many experts think they should be, nor does it mean that all cities have adequate enforcement machinery. But the point is that anti-slum codes have been in existence for many years and that model codes and enforcement guides are available to every city.[10] Few problems have been the subject of so much research and planning. The Federal Government and the State of New York joined in making an exhaustive local housing code study in 1955.[11] Codes and enforcement methods were surveyed in 19 cities in 14 states. In addition, 53 cities, towns, and villages in the State of New York were surveyed. As a result a three-volume report was made available to every city in the United States. One volume contains a model minimum housing standards code which even includes detailed legal and administrative forms; another is devoted to code enforcement problems and recommendations; and the third volume consists of an administrative guide for local

---

[7] *Id.*, p. 115.

[8] People ex rel. Copcutt v. Board of Health of the City of Yonkers, 140 N.Y. 1, 7, 35 N.E. 320, 321 (1893).

[9] *Report of the President's Advisory Committee on Government Housing Policies and Programs,* 1953, p. 108.

[10] See for example, "A Proposed Housing Ordinance" (New York: American Public Health Association) and "Provisions of Housing Codes in Various American Cities" (Washington: Government Printing Office).

[11] This was done under a federal grant of $96,000 and a state contribution of $48,300.

anti-slum programs.[12] Advice and assistance in code enforcement is available from a variety of private and governmental sources.

Housing codes usually included standards for minimum space per occupant, basic sanitary equipment and facilities, light, ventilation, heating equipment where climatic conditions warrant, and safe and sanitary maintenance of the building and all equipment. It has been well said that—

> Probably no single factor is as important in the over-all attack upon slums and blight as the enactment and enforcement of a Housing Code to establish minimum standards of health, safety, and decency in dwellings. Such housing codes are the principal means by which the spread of slums and blight can be prevented.
>
>   ❉   ❉   ❉
>
> The development and enforcement of city-wide codes, which are an expression of the local police power have a vital relationship to urban renewal projects. . . .[13]

Federal Legislation

Original Federal Program—an Unemployment Relief Measure —1933. As indicated above, the Federal Government first became engaged in slum clearance and the construction of public housing during the early 1930's as a part of the program to provide unemployment relief during the depression. The National Industrial Recovery Act of 1933 provided for such projects and other emergency public works "with a view to increasing employment quickly."[14] The Act stated that the Federal Government could acquire any real or personal property needed in connection with such projects "by exercise of the power of eminent domain."[15]

---

[12] These documents were made available by the Bureau of Community Development, State Housing Division, 270 Broadway, New York 7, N.Y. In 1956, the Urban Renewal Administration published a review of housing codes in 56 cities, and the code of the American Public Health Association. See *UR Bulletin,* No. 3, 1956.

[13] *Planning Urban Renewal Projects* (Washington: Chamber of Commerce of the United States, 1960), pp. 11-12.

[14] 48 Stat. 201, 202 (1933).

[15] 48 Stat. 202 (1933). It is not clear why the power to seize *personal* property was included unless it was felt that it might be necessary to seize the contents of slum dwellings as well as the realty.

The Act of 1933 also sought to stimulate construction of low-rent housing by providing loans to limited dividend corporations. But only seven limited dividend projects were initiated during the first year the program was in operation, and although $100 million was set aside for such projects only about 10 percent of it was used. The failure of this approach, of course, was due to the fact that there was little to attract cash equity in the way of return or safety.

Prior to direct federal involvement in slum clearance, President Hoover became concerned with the housing problem and following a national housing conference sponsored by him in 1931, the Congress authorized the Reconstruction Finance Corporation to make loans "to rebuild slum areas" and provide low-income housing.[16]

Direct Federal Slum Clearance Held Unconstitutional—1935. In 1935, the United States Court of Appeals for the Sixth Circuit sustained a lower court decision holding a federal slum clearance and public housing project in Louisville, Kentucky, unconstitutional. The opinion of the court of appeals stated that while the states have broad police powers to deal with such problems, "the federal government has no such power within the states." The taking of one citizen's property "for the purpose of improving it and selling or leasing it to another," the court concluded, "is not . . . within the scope of the powers of the federal government."[17] The Louisville case is discussed in greater detail at page 47, *infra*.

Substitution of Federal-Aid Approach—1937. In 1937 the grant-in-aid approach was substituted for direct federal slum clearance. The Congress directed that federally owned low-rent housing projects be sold or leased to local public housing agencies. The

---

[16] Following a Senate Committee report on building codes in 1921, Mr. Hoover, who was then Secretary of Commerce, set up a Building Code Committee within the Department of Commerce. The Committee issued eight reports recommending various local building code requirements. As early as 1892, Congress appropriated $20,000 for a Labor Department study of slum conditions in the larger cities. *Law and Contemporary Problems, op. cit.,* p. 97.

[17] United States v. Certain Lands in the City of Louisville, 78 F. 2d 684 (6th Cir. 1935), *appeal dismissed,* 297 U.S. 726 (1936).

United States Housing Act of 1937 provided loans, and federal grants not exceeding 25 percent of project cost, for slum clearance and low-rent housing.[18] Pursuant to the Act of 1937, which created the United States Housing Authority, a number of state laws were passed to create local housing authorities to acquire land by purchase or condemnation and construct, own, and operate low-rent housing projects subsidized by the Federal Government.

A Comprehensive Program Authorized—1949. Following extensive congressional hearings from time to time over a period of years, and various unsuccessful efforts to expand the Act of 1937, Congress enacted a greatly expanded slum clearance and redevelopment program as a part of the Housing Act of 1949.[19] Upon passage of the Act of 1949, federal housing authorities envisioned a "comprehensive attack" upon slums "for the first time in our history." The attack was to be made "by local communities," it was explained, with the Federal Government providing "the *leverage* that [the] cities have long needed to get their redevelopment programs going."[20] The Act of 1949 provides most of the basic authority and policy under which the present program operates.[21] The key features of the 1949 Act are summarized below.

National Objective and Policy. The national urban renewal program is based upon three assumptions: (1) that the general welfare of the Nation requires elimination of substandard housing; (2) that this cannot be done effectively unless public agencies acquire and clear large "blighted" areas for private redevelopment; and (3) that state and local governments lack the financial resources to handle "any substantial proportion" of the

---

[18] For a discussion of the grant-in-aid approach see p. 51.

[19] P.L. 171, 81st Congress.

[20] Housing and Home Finance Agency, *A Handbook of Information on Provisions of the Housing Act of 1949,* p. 1. Italics added. Ten years later, according to the latest available reports, final federal grants had been made for only 26 projects.

[21] The Act of 1949 has been amended from time to time. Significant changes made by the Housing Amendments of 1954, 1959, and 1961 are referred to at pp. 37-43.

areas involved. Among other things, the Act of 1949 declared that as a matter of national policy—

> . . . appropriate local bodies shall be encouraged and assisted to undertake positive programs of encouraging and assisting the development of well-planned, integrated residential neighborhoods, the development and redevelopment of communities. . . .

The Act also provided that federal assistance should be rendered "to eliminate substandard and other inadequate housing through the clearance of slums and blighted areas, . . ."[22]

Before approving financial assistance for a slum clearance project, the Administrator of the Housing and Home Finance Agency[24] was directed by the Act to "give consideration" to whether local authorities have adopted or modernized their housing codes, not to rehabilitate or eliminate *existing* slum properties, but to prevent "the spread or recurrence" of slums.

It should be noted here that the national policy as set forth in the Act of 1949, (1) is not confined to the elimination of "slums," but refers to elimination of *"substandard"* and other *"inadequate"* housing and the clearance of *"blighted"* areas, and, (2) makes no reference to the enforcement of local housing codes so as to require rehabilitation, or demolition if necessary, of slum properties by those legally responsible for such properties—their owners. In fact, by enumerating "Local Responsibilities" in another section of the Act (section 101) without reference to rehabilitation, the statute of 1949 could actually be construed as declaring a national policy *against* the local rehabilitation approach.[23]

Loans and Capital Grants. Under the 1949 authorization, federal lending authority aggregating $1 billion (outstanding at any one time) was provided for the following purposes:

---

[22] P.L. 171, 81st Congress, § 2.

[23] "Expressio unis est exclusio alterius." (The expression of one thing is the exclusion of another.)

[24] The Housing and Home Finance Agency was created in 1947 to coordinate various housing programs of the Federal Government. HHFA includes the Urban Renewal Administration and other agencies concerned with the urban renewal program. See organizational chart, p. 45.

(a) Preliminary surveys and plans by local public agencies.

(b) Assembling, clearing, preparing, and selling or leasing, the land in the project area.

(c) Construction of schools or other public facilities to serve or support a redeveloped area on open, or predominantly open, land.

(d) Long-term loans (up to 40 years) where the cleared property is to be leased instead of sold. It was provided that such loans would bear interest at the "going Federal rate" as defined in the Act. Shortly after passage of the Act this rate was determined to be about 2.5 percent a year.

In addition to lending authority, the 1949 Act authorized capital grants for slum clearance and redevelopment at the rate of $100 million per year for five years. Federal capital grants were made available to finance two-thirds of the "net project cost." This cost is the difference between the cost of the property to be cleared, demolition of the buildings, clearing, etc., and the amount received from the sale of the cleared land to private redevelopers. Although it is said that the city or other local authority must put up at least one-third of this net cost, the law provided that the local share would be reduced by amounts spent by the city, or local authority, on projects to serve or support the project area such as parks, schools, playgrounds, and public buildings. As this has worked out the federal share has actually averaged around 86 percent of project cost.[25]

A Hypothetical Project. The Housing and Home Finance Agency (HHFA) has described a hypothetical project under the Act of 1949 as follows:

> . . . First, the city wants to make certain a portion of the Federal funds is reserved for its use. Through a resolution of its city council it requests the Housing and Home Finance Administration to reserve capital grant funds for projects it intends to undertake. . . . The Administrator agrees. . . .
>
> Central City then takes the steps necessary to qualify for financial aid. It establishes a local public agency qualified to undertake slum clearance projects. It already has a city plan which fulfills the major

---

[25] See "How the Program Works," pp. 51-52.

requirements of a general plan. . . . It has already instituted positive programs to . . . [modernize] its building codes and other regulations and to prevent the spread and recurrence of slums and blight. . . . The city also has a tentative idea of the slum and blighted areas which it believes it can reasonably clear out. . . . It is ready to go into the slum clearance business.

Preliminary and final advances. Central City now needs funds for surveys necessary to define a project area. . . . Upon approval of the survey plans, the Administrator enters into a preliminary advance contract . . . by which the funds are made available.

The local public agency then conducts such surveys. . . . These surveys produce . . . additional data . . . as to the fulfillment of the requirement for relocating families in the area who will be displaced by clearance operations, for marketability of the land for redevelopment, the preliminary estimates of costs of the project, and other factors. It is then ready to complete the plans . . . so it submits . . . an application for a final advance of funds of $75,000 for detailed plans and surveys for the project. Upon approval of the application by the Administrator, a final advance contract is executed.

Temporary loan and grant contract. Some months later the local agency is ready to submit an application for a temporary loan and capital grant. . . . It has completed the . . . plan to be followed by redevelopers in rebuilding the area. It has a plan for rehousing families which will be displaced. . . . It has reasonable assurances as to the marketability of the land for the new uses. . . .

In addition, the local public agency can now show estimates of how much money it will need. . . . It also has assurance that Central City will contribute about $350,000 in donations of land, services in connection with project activities, and other public improvements, such as schools, playgrounds, parks, etc., which are necessary to serve the project area.

Cost estimates. The local agency estimates that the project will cost $1,650,000 (including the $100,000 it already has spent for surveys and plans), in addition to the $350,000 in local contributions, to acquire, clear, prepare the land, and make the area available for redevelopment. This makes a gross project cost of $2,000,000. The local agency estimates that the land will be sold for approximately $800,000. This means that the project will be approximately $1,200,000 in the red after it has been completed. Since the Federal capital grant on this project cannot exceed two-thirds of this deficit, the local share cannot be less than $400,000. The local agency, therefore, must agree to provide $50,000 in cash donations in addition to the $350,000 in land, services, and facilities which Central City has already pledged to donate to the project.

The local public agency's application thus requests a contract for a $1,650,000 Federal temporary loan to finance the undertaking of the project and for an $800,000 Federal capital grant to finance two-thirds of the deficit . . . the Administrator enters into a contract for a temporary loan and capital grant with the local public agency for the amounts requested. The local agency uses the proceeds of the loan first to pay the principal and interest due on the $100,000 advance received by the local agency, and then to acquire, clear and prepare the land for redevelopment and to sell the land to redevelopers. At the conclusion of the project, the $1,650,000 loan is repaid with the proceeds of the sale of the land, amounting to $800,000, the Federal capital grant, amounting to $800,000, and the local cash contribution of $50,000.[26]

The Act of 1949 does not require the localities to sell slum property for private redevelopment to the highest responsible competitive bidder despite the fact that the property is purchased with public funds and the Federal Government has the biggest stake in the sale price. At most, the local public slum clearance agency pays only one-third of the loss on such sales and in many cases much less. Considerable controversy has arisen from time to time as a result of sales of vast areas of city property to private redevelopers without competitive bidding.

Low Rent Public Housing. Public housing consists of housing subsidized by the Government and operated by local housing authorities. Federal loans are available for construction of projects and annual contributions are made to cover operating losses. During the early 1930's, 21,600 public housing units were constructed by the Public Works Administration and for some time were operated by the Federal Government itself. As noted above, the Act of 1937 provided for the transfer of such operations to local authorities. When the Act of 1949 was passed, 191,700 units of this kind were in operation. The 1949 statute extended the program by increasing public housing loan funds to $1.5 billion and authorizing annual contributions up to $308 million per year. Preference for occupancy of these units was given, first, to low-income families displaced by slum clearance and then to other low-income families. Veterans of World Wars I and

---

[26] See HHFA Handbook, *op. cit.,* p. 7, *et seq.*

II were placed at the top of each of these two groups. The principal rules for admission to public housing, under the Act of 1949, have been summarized by HHFA as follows:

1. The top rent for admission must be at least 20 percent below the rents at which private enterprise is providing a substantial supply of available standard housing, either new or old.
2. The net income of families at admission (less a $100 exemption for each minor member) cannot exceed five times the annual rent to be charged, including utilities.
3. Local authorities must set maximum income limits, both for admission to the project and for continued residence in it. These limits are subject to PHA approval.
4. The authority must make a written report to PHA showing that incomes of families admitted are within the limit.
5. The authority must reexamine the incomes of all tenant families periodically to adjust rents if necessary and to evict those families whose incomes have risen above the limit for continued occupancy.

The maximum income limits for admission are set by the authority after a careful study of local needs. Factors considered include the incomes of families forced to live in slum housing, the lowest incomes earned by regularly employed workers, and income levels permitted by relief agencies for their clients. Maximum income limits for continued occupancy are generally set 20 to 25 percent above the admission limits to allow some increase in family income without necessitating eviction.[27]

In order to obtain a loan or grant under the Act of 1949 the locality is required to agree that persons displaced by clearance operations will be provided with "decent, safe, and sanitary dwellings" at rents and prices within their financial means.[28] One of the purposes of federally subsidized public housing projects, of course, is to assist the localities in meeting this requirement. The locality must also agree—in order to obtain federally subsidized public housing units—that a "substantially equal" number of unsafe or unsanitary dwelling units will be eliminated.[29]

Commercial Redevelopment. In defining a "project" for which federal assistance could be obtained, the Act did not

[27] *Ibid.*, p. 12.
[28] 42 USCA § 1455(c).
[29] 42 USCA § 1410(a).

exclude commercial redevelopment of areas which were "predominantly residential in character" prior to clearance. In other words, a residential area could be cleared and redeveloped as a commercial area. But the Act required that where a commercial area—"*not* predominantly residential"—is cleared it must be redeveloped for "predominantly residential uses." In addition, the Act defined a project so as to include predominantly open land "which because of obsolete platting, diversity of ownership, deterioration of structures or of site improvements, or otherwise substantially impairs or arrests the sound growth of the community and which is to be developed for predominantly residential uses." Wholly open land could not be acquired with a federal grant, but loans were made available for acquisition of such property if "necessary for sound community growth" and if it is to be used for predominantly residential development.

Labor Standards. Under the 1949 statute, federal aid cannot be obtained unless the local authorities agree that the salaries of all architects, technical engineers, etc., engaged in development of the project, shall be "not less than the salaries prevailing in the locality." In the case of most other workers ("laborers and mechanics") they must be paid not less than the wages prevailing in the locality as predetermined in Washington by the Secretary of Labor. Monthly compliance reports to the Secretary of Labor were required of all project contractors and subcontractors.

State Enabling Laws. In order to meet the requirements of the Act of 1949, many states found it necessary to enact legislation authorizing local governmental units to participate in the new federal slum clearance and urban redevelopment program. In some states the new legislation required that the program be carried out by the established local housing authority; in other states each locality was given the choice of proceeding in this manner or establishing a separate redeveloping authority, and in still others the new laws prohibited the administration of such programs by a local housing authority thus making it impossible for a locality to participate without establishing a separate agency for that purpose. Today nearly all of the states have urban renewal enabling legislation and are participating in the federal program.[30]

"Redirection" of the Federal Program—1954. After 20 years of federal slum clearance activity and the expenditure of millions of dollars in public funds and nearly five years after the "comprehensive attack" was authorized in 1949, the President and many members of Congress began to take a second look at the whole basic philosophy of urban redevelopment legislation. The President appointed an Advisory Committee to study the problem. In December 1953, the President's Advisory Committee on Government Housing Policies and Programs found that the program was not getting at the real cause of slums and disclosed that slums were actually developing faster than they were being eliminated.[31] The Advisory Committee Report was followed up by extensive congressional hearings and "shirt sleeves" conferences held by the Housing and Home Finance Agency Administrator to obtain the advice of all groups interested in housing. In the light of these developments, Congress enacted the Housing Act of 1954 which, it was said, would "redirect" the federal slum clearance and redevelopment program. As explained by the Chairman of the Senate Committee[32] in charge of the 1954 amendments, they were designed primarily "to broaden and redirect the present programs . . . so as to assist not only the communities in clearing their slums, as is presently provided but to prevent their spread by *rehabilitating* and *improving* blighted, deteriorated, or deteriorating areas." And he also stated:

> What is sought to be done under the new section, in cooperation with the cities and the States, is to *rehabilitate* or *rebuild* the old houses and make them livable. . . . This section of the bill will become operative only when a city agrees to adopt acceptable ordinances and plans.[33]

---

[30] See bulletin entitled, *State Enabling Legislation,* Housing and Home Finance Agency, February 1, 1960.

[31] On November 24, 1953, Robert B. Mitchell, Consultant to the President's Advisory Committee, reported to the Committee that "we are producing slums faster than we can demolish them."

[32] Senator Capehart, then Chairman of the Committee on Banking and Currency.

[33] *Congressional Record,* June 3, 1954, pp. 7612-13. (Emphasis added.)

The "Workable Program" Requirement. The focal point of the legislative "redirection" of 1954 was a provision to make federal aid contingent upon adoption by the city involved of what is known as a "workable program." The workable program evolved from two statutes. The first was a "rider" on the HHFA appropriation bill of 1954. This required the Administrator of HHFA, before approving a slum-clearance program, "to consider the efforts of localities to enforce local codes relating to health, sanitation, and safety for dwellings, and the feasibility of achieving slum-clearance objectives through rehabilitation of existing dwellings and areas." This provision also stated that FHA authority to insure loans for repair and alteration must be used "to the utmost" in connection with rehabilitation needs.[34]

The intent of this requirement seemed reasonably clear and simple: the Administrator should *not* approve a federal subsidy for seizure, demolition, and clearance of "substandard" dwellings without first considering the feasibility of rehabilitating them and he should promote slum-clearance objectives by rehabilitation whenever feasible. In order to assist the owners of such properties to comply with local code standards, Federal Housing Administration (FHA) insurance of loans for repairs and alterations was to be "used to the utmost." In reporting the bill which became the Housing Act of 1954, the Senate Committee on Banking and Currency stated that it contained an amendment under which this provision would be repealed and "the effect of these provisos . . . incorporated" in the basic slum clearance statute.[35] The new language provided that no contract could be entered into for a federal capital grant, loan, or annual public housing subsidy unless—

(1) there is presented to the Administrator by the locality a workable program (which shall include an official plan of action, as it exists from time to time, for effectively dealing with the problem of urban slums and blight within the community and for the establishment and preservation of a well-planned community with

[34] As described in Senate Report 1472, 83d Congress, 2d Session, May 28, 1954, pp. 76-77.
[35] *Ibid.*

well-organized residential neighborhoods of decent homes and suitable living environment for adequate family life)

[a] for utilizing appropriate private and public resources to eliminate, and prevent the development or spread of, slums and urban blight,

[b] to encourage needed urban rehabilitation,

[c] to provide for the redevelopment of blighted, deteriorated, or slum areas, or

[d] to undertake such of the aforesaid activities or other feasible community activities as may be suitably employed to achieve the objectives of such a program.[36]

The Act of 1954 provided further that the authority to certify local workable programs as meeting these requirements prior to approval of federal aid could not be delegated but must be exercised by the HHFA Administrator personally.

If the workable program section was intended to incorporate the effect of the repealed provision so as to require rehabilitation of salvable property by code enforcement as a condition to federal aid, its draftsmen were apparently unaware of this purpose. Literally, it merely requires "a *plan* of action"; the plan must be "workable" but it need not be actually working; it should provide for the use of "appropriate" private and public resources, but "appropriate" is not defined, and in any event, it need only "encourage" rehabilitation. The city is merely required to give assurance that it will undertake those parts of the plan which may be "suitably employed" to achieve program objectives.

---

[36] P.L. 560, 83d Congress, August 2, 1954, section 303. The "workable program" requirement apparently does not apply to federal grants to metropolitan, state, and regional planning agencies. Planning grants, under legislation approved in 1959, were limited to $20 million. However, the Housing Act of 1961 increased this authorization to $75 million and increased the federal contribution for planning projects from one-half to two-thirds of the cost of such work. It is estimated that only a very small percentage of the localities have adopted "workable programs" before receiving planning grants.

Federally subsidized renewal planning, which is generally performed under contracts with private consultants, has been criticized on the ground that many such plans are unrealistically expensive—that they envision "dream cities"—and that a substantial number of them never reach the project stage.

It appears, also, that loans for community facilities—water and sewer lines, etc.—are not subject to the "workable program" requirement.

Although the Senate Report on the bill of 1954 assured the Congress that the effect of the appropriation bill provisos was "incorporated" in the bill, elsewhere the Report left little doubt that whatever teeth it had had been extracted. While stating on one hand that "any community that defaults on its own program, through laxity or indifference should forfeit its right to continued Federal assistance" it is made clear elsewhere that this means "assistance for *future* projects" and that disbursement of funds for a project after an assistance agreement is entered into "should not be contingent upon specific demonstration of progress in carrying out the workable program."[37]

In its report on the bill of 1954, the Senate Committee stated that the bill provided funds for clearance of *"rock bottom slum areas"* and that effective local action should be taken "for the conservation and rehabilitation of blighted areas which economically are still worth saving."[38] But the bill as finally enacted contains no such language. Instead, grants and loans are made available for "urban renewal" including demolition and clearance of standard as well as substandard structures so long as they are in "deteriorated or deteriorating" areas.[39] In other words, the Act itself, in effect, emphasized condemnation, clearance, and redevelopment while minimizing conservation and rehabilitation measures.

Rehabilitation Loans. The Act also added section 220 to the National Housing Act to provide FHA mortgage insurance for rehabilitation of dwellings as well as the construction of new ones in urban renewal areas. Insurance of advances under open-end mortgages was also authorized. Such mortgages provide that the outstanding balance can be increased to provide additional loan funds for improvements, alterations and repairs without executing a new mortgage. One of the principal purposes of section 220, of course, is to assist owners who are ordered to rehabilitate their properties to comply with anti-slum code stand-

---

[37] Senate Report 1472, *op. cit.; U. S. Code: Congressional and Administrative News*, 1954, Vol. 2, p. 2759.

[38] *Ibid.*, p. 2762.

[39] The Housing Act of 1954, P.L. 560, 83d Congress, § 311.

ards. However, in actual practice its use has been extensively in connection with construction of new rental housing often in the semi-luxury class.

Relocation Housing. Section 221 was another addition to the National Housing Act effected by the Housing Act of 1954. This provides a high risk type of mortgage insurance designed to facilitate the purchase of new or existing dwelling units by families being displaced by various forms of governmental action including urban renewal. Section 221 mortgage insurance is also available for construction of *rental* housing operated primarily for the benefit of those who are relocated.

FNMA Special Assistance. In order to assure the availability of mortgage money for urban renewal projects and relocation housing, the 1954 Act authorized the Federal National Mortgage Association to purchase loans initiated by private lenders. This form of special assistance, which is in actuality a form of direct lending, made possible many projects for which permanent private financing could not have been found.

The Housing Act of 1959. The Housing Act of 1959 further liberalized the urban renewal program in a variety of ways. Among other things, the 1959 Act—

1. Provided that the President could authorize urban renewal loan contracts outstanding at any one time in excess of the previous $1 billion limitation.

2. Authorized an increase in maximum relocation payments from $100 to $200 for individuals displaced by urban renewal and certain other public activities.

3. Provided that a locality's share of the cost of an urban renewal project may be reduced by the cost of its public improvements such as parks, playgrounds, and public buildings in the renewal area where such improvements were made within three years prior to signing a loan and grant contract. Provision was also made for crediting the local share, under certain circumstances, with acquisition and clearance expenditures by institutions of higher learning

where such expenditures are made within five years prior to the federal aid contract.

4. Authorized federal assistance for 35,000 additional units of low-rent public housing.

The Housing Act of 1961. The Act of 1961[40] authorized further expansion and liberalization of the urban renewal program. Among other things, the 1961 amendments—

1. Increased the grant authorization for urban renewal from $2 billion to $4 billion. $25 million of such grants may be used for mass transportation demonstration projects.

2. Provides that relocation payments to business concerns displaced by urban redevelopment may equal their total certified actual moving expenses even though the expenses are in excess of the limit of $3,000. The additional payments will be made by the Federal Government. Also, authorizes loans to small businesses which have suffered substantial economic injury as a result of displacement by federally aided urban renewal or highway construction programs or by any other construction conducted by or with funds provided by the Federal Government. The loans will bear an interest rate of not more than the higher of (1) 2¾ percent or (2) the average annual interest rate on all interest-bearing obligations of the United States plus one-fourth of one percent (currently a rate of 3.5 percent).

3. Permits local public agencies to carry out rehabilitation demonstrations in urban renewal projects by acquiring properties, improving them for dwelling use or related facilities, and reselling them to private owners.

4. Increases the amount of grant authorization which may be used for nonresidential purposes from 20 to 30 percent. The Act of 1959 increased the maximum from 10 to 20 percent. Increases the permissible amount of capital grants from two-thirds to three-fourths of net project cost in cities

---

[40] Public Law 87-70, approved June 30, 1961. See Section-by-Section Summary of P.L. 87-70, Committee Print, U.S. Senate, Committee on Banking and Currency, p. 7.

having a population of 50,000 or less—150,000 or less in an economically distressed area.

5. Authorizes grants aggregating up to $50 million to states and local public bodies to help finance the acquisition of open-space land.

6. Authorizes contributions to public housing projects so as to permit contracts for construction of an additional 100,000 public housing units. Also gives localities greater flexibility in determining requirements for admission to public housing subsidized by the Federal Government.

7. Increased previous ceiling on amounts which may be appropriated for urban planning grants from $20 million to $75 million, and federal financing of such a project from one-half to two-thirds of the estimated cost of the work.

8. Provides a special FHA-insured repair loan program for urban renewal areas. Loans may be for a 20-year term and up to $10,000.

9. Broadens the FHA relocation insurance program under section 221 to include a special class of rental housing to be subsidized by omission of the FHA insurance premium, and by provisions for financing with special low interest rate loans. The new Act also provides for purchase and use of urban renewal project land for moderate income rental or cooperative housing at prices below those heretofore considered fair value. The rate of such loans is currently set at $3\frac{1}{8}$ percent which makes them unacceptable to private investors. It is therefore expected they will be purchased by FNMA with special funds provided for that purpose by the 1961 Act. Mortgagors are limited to certain public agencies and nonprofit groups.

10. Provides for refinancing existing redevelopment projects under the provisions of 9 above when it is found that such action will facilitate occupancy by persons of low or moderate income.

Summary. Federal legislation dealing with slum clearance and public housing was first enacted as a part of the unemployment relief program in the 1930's. The original direct federal approach was declared unconstitutional in 1935. However, federal participation was continued under a federal subsidy arrangement which operated on a relatively limited basis until Congress authorized a "comprehensive" program in 1949. The federal aid program was broadened and "redirected" in 1954, one of the objectives being to bring private enterprise into urban renewal by providing financing which would be attractive to private redevelopers interested in profit-making ventures. Among the significant innovations of subsequent legislation is that introduced by the 1961 Act providing special subsidies for certain public agencies and private nonprofit groups designed to encourage them to build and operate rental housing for occupancy by low and moderate income families. In the event this stimulates public redevelopment as planned, it may well discourage investment and participation by private enterprise—participation which the Act of 1954 sought to encourage.

The principal federal agencies involved in the administration of urban renewal laws are shown in the chart on the following page.

Federal Agencies Involved In Urban Renewal

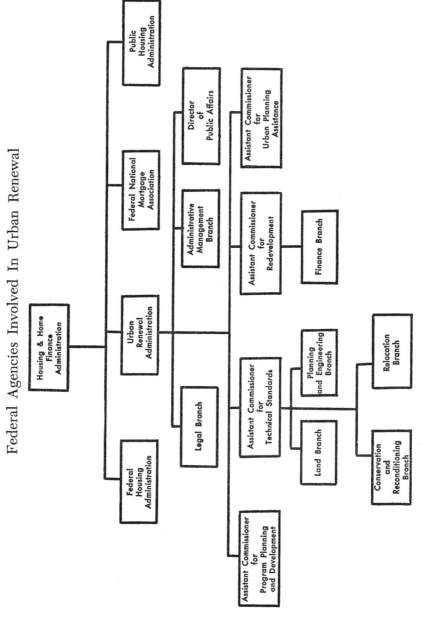

Source: Fourteenth Annual Report of the Housing and Home Finance Agency, 1960.

[45]

CHAPTER IV

The Federal Program and Constitutional Concepts

Introduction

Revolutions in Governmental Policy. The constitutional concepts underlying urban renewal have evolved from at least two revolutions in governmental policy. "The first revolution," it has been said, "began with the breakup of the feudal system."[1] This "revolutionary" doctrine, of course, was that real property should not be held "at the pleasure of the Crown." The elder William Pitt epitomized the 18th century concept of private property when he said:

> . . . The poorest man may in his cottage bid defiance to all the forces of the Crown. It may be frail; its roof may shake; the wind may blow through it; the storms may enter, the rain may enter, but the King of England cannot enter; all his forces dare not cross the threshold of the ruined tenement.

During the same era, Blackstone, in his *Commentaries,* was more specific: "Regard of the law for private property is so great," he wrote, "that it will not authorize the least violation of it, not even for the general good of the whole community; for it would be dangerous to allow any private man, or even any public tribunal, to be the judge of this common good. . . ."[2]

In this country the right to own private property has always been associated with freedom. Early in our history private property was not merely regarded in a materialistic sense—"It became the supreme symbol of individual freedom and of the protection of the individual in his freedom."[3] The recent seizures of prop-

---

[1] Miles L. Colean, "Changing Attitudes Toward Property Ownership and Mortgage Finance," *Law and Contemporary Problems, op. cit.,* p. 25.

[2] *Blackstone's Commentaries* (Ewell Ed. 1889), p. 26.

[3] *Ibid.* See also William Henry Chamberlin, "Right to Own," *The Wall Street Journal,* August 15, 1960.

erty in Cuba, denounced here as "economic banditry," point up the basic difference between our traditional concepts and those of various totalitarian regimes. Article VI of the Soviet Constitution, for example, provides that "The land . . . and the bulk of the dwelling houses in the cities and industrial localities are state property, . . ."[4] Under our Constitution it was understood at the outset that a man was free to use his property as he pleased so long as its use did not interfere with the rights of others and that the Government could not take private property except "for public use."[5] There can be little doubt that this concept had a tremendous influence, perhaps as much as any other single factor, upon the phenomenal expansion and development of America as a wealthy and free society.

As noted in Chapter III, the second revolution, with which we are primarily concerned, began during the depression of the 1930's. In its efforts to create employment, the Federal Government reached into the sphere of traditional state jurisdiction, seized private properties in various cities, and entered directly into local slum clearance and the construction of housing for low-income groups. It was said that traditional private property concepts must not stand in the way of "broader social objectives." The federal program, which began as a temporary unemployment relief measure, has not only survived for over 25 years; it has developed into a multi-billion dollar activity and the Congress has seriously considered the creation of a permanent cabinet Department of Urban Affairs and Housing for the principal purpose of handling its operations.

ORIGINAL FEDERAL APPROACH

The Louisville Case. As pointed out in Chapter III, the original federal approach to slum clearance suffered a temporary setback when it was declared unconstitutional in 1935. The original program made no pretense of merely "aiding" the states. The Federal Government itself sent its representatives into selected

---

[4] As quoted by Senator Strom Thurmond, *Congressional Record,* February 5, 1959, p. 1757.

[5] Constitution of the United States, Amendment V.

cities, took title to the properties involved, demolished the buildings thereon, and constructed its own low-cost housing. By 1935, work had begun on projects of this kind, apparently without challenge in the courts, in at least 15 cities. However, when the Federal Government sought to condemn four city blocks for a project in Louisville, Kentucky, one of the property owners went into federal court and challenged its power to do so. The lower federal court held for the property owner and the Government appealed to the United States Court of Appeals for the Sixth Circuit. From what provision of the Constitution, the Government was asked, did it derive the power to take private homes and replace them with housing for rent to low-income groups? The Government cited the constitutional provision empowering the Congress to levy taxes to "provide for the . . . general welfare of the United States." It argued that "this power carries with it the right to acquire property by condemnation upon which Congress may expend tax funds."[6] But, regardless of how broad the power to tax and spend may be, the court of appeals pointed out, the Fifth Amendment restricts the federal condemnation power to takings "for public use." Was the Louisville property to be taken "for public use" in a national sense, and, in any event, are funds for a local slum clearance project used for the "*general* welfare of the *United States*"? The court thought not.

Even assuming that such a project could be considered a use for the benefit of the general public within the state or city, the court observed that "what is a public use under one sovereign may not be a public use under another." The states have broad "police powers" to deal with matters affecting the health, morals, and welfare of their people, the court stated, but "the Federal Government has no such power *within* the states."[7]:

> . . . The tearing down of the old buildings and the construction of new ones on the land here sought to be taken would create, it is true, a new resource for the employment of labor and capital. It is likewise true that the erection of new sanitary dwellings upon the property and the leasing or the selling of them at low prices would

---

[6] United States v. Certain Lands in the City of Louisville, 78 F. 2d (6th Cir. 1935), *appeal dismissed*, 297 U.S. 726 (1936).

[7] *Id.* at 687.

enable many residents of the community to improve their living conditions. It may be, too, that these group benefits, so far as they might affect the general public, would be beneficial. If, however, such a result thus attained is to be considered a public use for which the government may condemn private property, there would seem to be no reason why it could not condemn any private property which it could employ to an advantage to the public.

And the court continued:

. . . There are perhaps many properties that the government could use for the benefit of selected groups. It might be, indeed, that by acquiring large sections of the farming parts of the country and leasing the land or selling it at low prices it could advance the interest of many citizens of the country, or that it could take over factories and other businesses and operate them upon plans more beneficial to the employees or the public, or even operate or sell them at a profit to the government to the relief of the taxpayers. The public interest that would thus be served, however, cannot, we think, be held to be a public use for which the government, in the exercise of its governmental functions, can take private property.[8]

"The taking of one citizen's property for the purpose of improving it and selling or leasing it to another," the court concluded, "is not, in our opinion, within the scope of the powers of the federal government."

Following the decision of the court of appeals in 1935, the Federal Government filed a petition for certiorari (request for review) in the United States Supreme Court. However, before the case came up for argument in 1936, the Government decided against a Supreme Court test. The Louisville project was apparently abandoned and the petition was dismissed.[9] Federal seizures of property for such projects were discontinued and so it was said that "as a practical matter" the question of direct federal condemnations for slum clearance "had become moot."[10]

---

[8] *Id.*, at 688.

[9] 297 U.S. 726 (1936).

[10] As explained in United States v. Boyle, 52 F. Supp. (N.D. Ohio, 1943), *aff'd*, 323 U.S. 329 (1945). Prior to the dismissal of the Government's petition for review of the Louisville case in 1936, properties for 49 slum clearance projects in various cities were acquired by the Government.

United States vs. Local Code Enforcement—Oklahoma Case.
The impact of the Federal Government's original slum clearance
and low-income housing program on traditional local powers—
indeed upon enforcement of local anti-slum building codes—was
strikingly illustrated in a situation which arose in Oklahoma City.
The Government purchased a site and started construction of a
low-rent housing project. City authorities attempted to inspect
the construction work and to enforce the local building codes and
ordinances customarily applied to other construction of this character. The federal contractor contended that compliance with
local requirements would increase the cost of the project and,
acting upon official advice from Washington, he refused to comply. He was arrested, found guilty by the municipal court in
Oklahoma City, fined, and warned that he would be prosecuted
separately for each and every day that he continued construction
without compliance with local law. The federal contractor then
went into federal court in Oklahoma City and asked that local
authorities be enjoined from arresting him or enforcing the local
requirements. The federal court issued such an injunction and the
City and its officers appealed. But the appeal was to no avail. *The
injunction against enforcement of the City code was sustained.*[11]

It has been held also that low-rent projects constructed under
the original program were not subject to state, county, or municipal taxation.[12] Exemption of various types of property from local
taxation, it has been said, might well weaken the financial sound-
ness of local governmental units.

---

[11] Oklahoma City v. Sanders, 94 F. 2d, 323 (10th Cir. 1938). In this
decision the court stated, *inter alia*, that "it may be that some parts of
the nation may not immediately feel the benefits of such [slum clear-
ance] activity, but the increasing of employment and stimulation of
industry, and reducing illness, disease, and crime, has a beneficial
effect upon the nation as a whole and promotes the public welfare."
However, the Oklahoma case did not involve federal power to *condemn* property for slum clearance and public housing—an essential
feature of the original program. In this case the property involved
was *purchased* by the Government.

[12] Cleveland v. United States, 323 U.S. 329 (1945).

As explained earlier,[13] after the direct federal slum clearance and public housing program was declared unconstitutional it was replaced in 1937 by a "federal-aid" system which ultimately became the Urban Renewal Program. Federal authorities picture urban renewal as "essentially a local undertaking" to which the National Government offers "a helping hand." They state that "the initiative comes from local government" and that Congress has "firmly established" the principle that the national program is "not to supplant local effort and resources or to replace local responsibility and determination."[14] The Federal Government itself no longer condemns property for private redevelopment; local powers are used for this. The federal agency, according to the Urban Renewal Administration, "normally avoids superimposing its judgment on that of the local authorities, *except* with respect to policies and procedures that are necessary for successful administration of a Nation-wide program."[15] All that the Federal Government does, it is said, in effect, is to aid the localities in carrying out their "local responsibilities."

How the Program Works. After a project is planned under the guidance of the Urban Renewal Administration, the locality applies for a temporary loan to finance the project until it receives a "capital grant." Such grants, it is said, cover two-thirds (three-fourths in cities of 50,000 or less) of the "net project cost."[16] But under the grant formula, as it actually works out, the remaining one-third of the net cost is also defrayed by the Federal Government to the extent of local cost for certain work and improvements in the area. These improvements include parks, playgrounds, public buildings, and other public facilities. In fact, local costs can be credited to reduce the local contribution although the construction of such improvements was commenced

---

[13] Chapter III, p. 22.

[14] See HHFA, *Aids to Your Community*, pp. 3, 7, and statement of Urban Renewal Commissioner Walker, *The Evening Star* (Washington), August 18, 1960.

[15] *The Evening Star, op. cit.* (Emphasis added.)

[16] For an explanation of "net project cost" see p. 32.

as long as three years before the federal project was even author-
ized.[17] As pointed out by former President Eisenhower—

> . . . cities can count streets and other local improvements, *which they had already intended to construct,* as a part of their share of the costs of an urban renewal project. . . . As it is, the local cash contribution has averaged only about 14 percent of the cost of acquiring and preparing a project site for development. . . .[18]

Under the urban renewal provisions of federal law, a city cannot receive a capital grant or loan unless it adopts a "workable program" acceptable to and certified by the Administrator of the Housing and Home Finance Agency (HHFA). Moreover, a "workable program" as defined by federal law is not merely a program for clearance and redevelopment of the area. It must include an "official plan of action"—

(1) ". . . for effectively dealing with the problem of urban slums and blight within the community. . . ."

(2) ". . . for establishment and preservation of a well-planned community with well-organized residential neighborhoods of decent homes and suitable living environment for adequate family life. . . ."

(3) ". . . for utilizing appropriate private and public resources to eliminate, and prevent the development or spread of, slums and urban blight, . . ."

(4) ". . . to encourage needed urban rehabilitation, . . ."

(5) ". . . to provide for the redevelopment of blighted, deteriorated, or slum areas or

(6) ". . . to undertake such of the aforesaid activities or other feasible community activities as may be suitably employed to achieve the objectives of such a program, . . ."[19]

In addition, the city must agree that wage rates for those engaged in the development of the project will be not less than

---

[17] Section 414(a) of the Housing Act of 1959 (P.L. 86-372).

[18] Message to Congress, *Congressional Record,* July 7, 1959, p. 11689. (Emphasis added.)

[19] Section 101(c), Housing Act of 1949, as amended, 42 USCA § 1451(c).

those "prevailing in the locality" *as predetermined by the Secretary of Labor.*[20]

Other requirements include arrangements by the locality for relocation of families displaced from the renewal area. Government loans and annual contributions to provide low-rent housing for such persons are available through the Public Housing Administration. Here again, local authorities must comply with certain federal standards one of which relates to the selection of low-income groups who may occupy such units. Rent schedules, which are based upon the ability of the particular family to pay, are also subject to federal approval.[21]

Of course, the Federal Government cannot order a locality to participate in a renewal project, but the price of its failure to accept Washington's "helping hand" is the loss of renewal grants from the federal treasury to which its own taxpayers have contributed their lawful share.

"Persuasion" or *"Coercion"?* In 1936, just a few months after direct federal slum clearance was declared unconstitutional in the Louisville case, the indirect federal subsidy concept was invalidated also by the Supreme Court in the celebrated case of *United States* v. *Butler.*[22] That case involved "benefit payments" for farmers who would agree to reduce their crops as provided in the Agricultural Adjustment Act. Such payments were denied those who would not do so. As in the Louisville slum clearance case, the Government relied upon its power to tax and appropriate "for the general welfare." It was argued that compliance was not

---

[20] This applies to "laborers and mechanics" (which includes most workers except professional and clerical personnel) engaged in urban renewal work financed in whole or in part with federal funds. A similar provision requires that architects, engineers, etc., be paid prevailing salaries as determined by the Administrator of HHFA "subsequent to a determination under applicable State or local law."

[21] See *Low Rent Public Housing,* p. 34. The median monthly gross rent of all families admitted during the first half of 1959 was $39 per month. Annual federal contributions to keep existing projects operating during the fiscal year ending June 30, 1960, amounted to $131,188,377. (*Annual Report of the Housing and Home Finance Agency* [Washington: 1960], pp. 211, 220.)

[22] 297 U.S. 1 (1936).

compulsory—that the objective was being obtained through "voluntary cooperation." But to accept the Government's position, the Supreme Court said, "would be to shut our eyes to what all others . . . can see. . . . *The regulation is not in fact voluntary.* The farmer, of course, may refuse to comply, but the price of such refusal is the loss of benefits. . . . This is coercion by economic pressure. The asserted power of choice is illusory."[23] "At best," the Court said, "*it is a scheme for purchasing with federal funds submission to federal regulation of a subject reserved to the states.*"[24]

The issue of federal coercion arose again in 1937; this time in a much more complex setting.[25] Congress had authorized federal grants to the states for various programs including administration of unemployment compensation. Each type of grant depended upon state compliance with conditions prescribed by federal authority. It also imposed an unemployment compensation tax on employers. The tax could be reduced, however, by 90 percentum of amounts contributed to an unemployment fund under a state law *approved by federal authorities as meeting certain federal requirements.* But at that time there were no such state laws and, as pointed out by Mr. Justice Butler, when the unemployment tax provision was passed—

> Federal agencies prepared and took draft bills to state legislatures to enable and induce them to pass laws providing for unemployment compensation in accordance with Federal requirements. . . .[26]

Based upon the AAA decision rendered just a year previously, it was argued that the tax credit provision, conditioned upon the passage of prescribed state laws, amounted to federal coercion of the states in a field outside the scope of federal power. But the Supreme Court, in a five-to-four decision, upheld the Act. As Mr. Donald Richberg put it: "Five learned Justices, without visibly grinning, solemnly held that the taxpayer is not coerced by the

---

[23] United States v. Butler, 297 U.S. 1, 72 (1936). (Emphasis added.)
[24] *Ibid.*
[25] Steward Machine Co. v. Davis, 301 U.S. 548 (1937).
[26] Dissenting opinion. *Id.* at 618.

Federal Government. . . and that the state is not coerced because it 'voluntarily' enacts a state law."[27]

It is true, the Court said in the compensation case, that Congress cannot "coerce" the states in fields reserved to them. But, "for all that appears," the Court observed, the state involved (Alabama) "is satisfied with her choice." In the course of its opinion, the Court said that under the circumstances the "inducement or persuasion" involved did not go beyond the bounds of federal power. "In the tender of this [tax] credit," the opinion states, "Congress does not intrude upon fields foreign to its function. The purpose of its intervention, as we have shown, is to safeguard its own treasury and as an incident to that protection to place the states upon a footing of equal opportunity. Drains upon its own resources are to be checked; obstructions to the freedom of the states are to be leveled."[28]

Various states have come to realize that the strings attached to federal aid, whether labeled "persuasion" or "coercion," are very effective indeed. Federal law, for example, requires state and local officials connected with activities financed wholly or *in part* by federal loans or grants to abstain from taking "any active part in political management or campaigns."[29] The State of Oklahoma tested this provision when a federal agency ordered it to remove a member of its State Highway Commission. The federal agency had determined that the State Commissioner should be removed from office because of his participation in a dinner to raise funds for the Democratic party. In upholding the removal demand the Supreme Court acknowledged that the State must comply or forfeit a part of its federal highway allotment, but it is "not

---

[27] "Should We Revive the Constitution?", *American Bar Association Journal*, January 1952, p. 86.

[28] 301 U.S. 548, 590-591 (1937). In discussing obstacles to the "freedom of the states" to impose an unemployment compensation tax voluntarily, the Court took the view that "many [states] held back through alarm lest in laying such a toll upon their industries, they would place themselves in a position of economic disadvantage as compared with neighbors or competitors. . . ." *Id.* at 588.

[29] 18 USCA § 1(a).

unusual," the Court said, for the Government to offer grants "dependent upon *cooperation* by the State with federal plans."[30]

Moreover, federal authorities have not only ordered state governments receiving federal aid to remove officials from office, but have ordered that such state officers not be rehired by *other* state or local agencies within a period of 18 months. When an agency in Ohio, for example, hired an official within 18 months after a federal agency ordered his removal from another state agency under federal orders, the State's federal funds were reduced and the reduction order was upheld by a United States District Court.[31]

Impact Upon State Concepts—Eminent Domain. By 1947, the total area-wide clearance approach had gained considerable support. "The mood is not simply to pick out the individual bad dwellings, but to tear down the whole neighborhood and make it over again. Don't fuss to enforce compliance with revised [antislum] standards; build new decent homes wholesale."[32] State and local power to eliminate slum conditions by requiring the *owners* of properties to maintain them in decent condition was well established, but could a state or local agency take property from one private owner, clear it, and then sell it to another for private redevelopment? There was a time when the Supreme Court had no hesitancy in asserting that—

> . . . The taking by a state of the private property of one person or corporation, without the owner's consent, for the private use of another, is not due process of law, and is a violation of the 14th Article of Amendment of the Constitution of the United States.[33]

[30] Oklahoma v. United States Civil Service Commission, 330 U.S. 127, 144 (1947). (Italics added.)

[31] Ohio v. United States Civil Service Commission, 65 F. Supp. 776 (S.D. Ohio, 1946). Federal demands take various forms. Last year, for example, the State of Louisiana was threatened with a proposal by federal authorities to cut off grants totaling $22 million a year unless the State changed its standards of eligibility for relief payments. *The New York Times*, November 15, 1960, p. 42.

[32] Shirley Adelson Siegel, "Real Property and Mass Housing Needs," *Law and Contemporary Problems, op. cit.*, p. 36.

[33] Missouri Pacific Ry. v. Nebraska, 164 U.S. 403 (1896). The Court invalidated a state agency order directing a railroad to permit the use of a suitable site along its right-of-way for erection of a grain elevator to be used by an association of farmers.

The constitutional test of state power to take property for urban redevelopment continues to be whether it is taken "for public use,"[34] but as Mr. Justice Holmes once said, "words are flexible."[35] Over the years, the words "for public *use*" have come to mean "for the public benefit," or "welfare."[36] In fact, the Supreme Court has said, in effect, that they mean whatever Congress or a state legislature says they mean.[37] The Court takes the view that "it is the function of Congress to decide what type of taking is for public use."[38] "In such cases," the Court said in 1946, "the legislature, not the judiciary, is the main guardian of the public needs to be served by social legislation. . . ."[39]

The ultimate impact of urban renewal upon the constitutional concept that one's property may not be taken by any governmental authority except "for public use" was spelled out in an opinion by Mr. Justice Douglas speaking for the Supreme Court in the case of *Berman* v. *Parker*.[40] The case involved the acquisition and redevelopment of an area 15 blocks square in what is known as "Area B" in the District of Columbia. A survey by the District Planning Commission indicated that over 38 percent of the dwellings in the area (and an unspecified percentage of the commercial properties) were either "satisfactory";[41] or merely needed "some major repairs."[42] The owners of a department store in Area B challenged the District's power to take it for redevelopment. One of the arguments of the store owners (appellants) was summarized by the Supreme Court as follows:

---

[34] United States Constitution, Amendment V.

[35] International Stevedoring Co. v. Haverty, 272 U.S. 50, 58 (1926).

[36] For a full discussion of this development see Coleman Woodbury, *Urban Development Problems and Practices* (Chicago: University of Chicago Press, 1953), p. 463, et. seq. (Italics added.)

[37] See Berman v. Parker, 348 U.S. 26 (1954).

[38] United States ex rel. T.V.A. v. Welch, 327 U.S. 546 (1946). This prompted Mr. Justice Reed, joined by Chief Justice Stone, to protest that under such a doctrine "an administrative agency could invoke a so-called political power so as to immunize its action against judicial examination in contests between the agency and the citizen."

[39] Berman v. Parker, *supra*.

[40] *Ibid*.

[41] *Ibid*.

[42] Opinion of the lower court, 117 F. Supp. 705 (D.C., 1953).

Appellants own property in Area B. . . . It is not used as a dwelling or place of habitation. A department store is located on it. Appellants object to the appropriation of this property for the purposes of the project. They claim that their property may not be taken constitutionally for this project. It is commercial, not residential property; it is not slum housing; it will be put into the project under the management of a private, not a public, agency and redeveloped for private, not public, use. That is the argument. . . . To take for the purpose of ridding the area of slums is one thing; it is quite another, the argument goes, to take a man's property merely to develop a better balanced, more attractive community.[43]

The lower court, composed of three federal judges, pointed out that the Consitution does not prevent the District of Columbia, or a state, from regulating slum dwellings even to the point of ordering them demolished, and that the land itself can be taken if *necessary* to eliminate a slum. But, as the opinion also points out, "a slum is made up of houses . . . and people. . . . The land itself neither contributes to nor detracts from a slum." "Ordinarily," the court observed, "the seizure of the fee title to land would seem to be neither necessary nor reasonably incidental to the clearance of a slum."

The following excerpts from the opinion of the lower federal court in *Berman* v. *Parker,* when contrasted with the Supreme Court's treatment of the case, discussed below, illustrates the ultimate impact of urban renewal upon the traditional concept of eminent domain:

> . . . we have the problem of the area which is not a slum but which is out of date, called by the Government "blighted" or "deteriorated." The Government says the statute is not limited to slum clearance but extends to what is called "urban redevelopment."
>
> ❋   ❋   ❋
>
> The hypothesis . . . is an urban area which does not breed disease or crime, [and] is not a slum. Its fault is that it fails to meet what are called modern standards. Let us suppose that it is backward, stagnant, not properly laid out, economically Eighteenth Century—anything except detrimental to health, safety or morals. Suppose its owners and occupants like it that way. Suppose they are old-fashioned, prefer single-family dwellings. . . . Or suppose these

---

[43] 348 U.S. 26, 31 (1954).

people own these homes and can afford none more modern. *The poor are entitled to own what they can afford. . . .*

❖   ❖   ❖

. . . There is no more subtle means of transforming the basic concepts of our government, of shifting from the preeminence of individual rights to the preeminence of government wishes, than is afforded by redefinition of "general welfare," as that term is used to define the Government's power of seizure. . . .

We are of opinion that the Congress, in legislating for the District of Columbia, has no power to authorize the seizure by eminent domain of property for the sole purpose of redeveloping the area according to its, or its agents, judgment of what a well-developed, well-balanced neighborhood would be. . . .

This concerns a situation where the plan is to redevelop an area upon only a part of which slums exist. . . . In essence the claim is that if slums exist the Government may seize, redevelop and sell all the property in any area it may select as appropriate, *so long as the area includes the slum area.* This amounts to a claim on the part of the authorities for unreviewable power to seize and sell whole sections of the city.

❖   ❖   ❖

The key to the plan, apart from slum clearance, is the opinion of the Government authorities that residential neighborhoods should be "well-balanced" and that the area should contain housing for all income groups. . . . The plan says: "The purpose of redevelopment is to clear the slums and replace them with that pattern of land use most appropriate to the overall development of the community."

No acute housing shortage is to be met. In fact the plan provides for no more residents than presently occupy the area. No pressing economic condition, apart from the slums, is sought to be dealt with by this plan. No purpose of housing for the needy—low-rent housing —is the motivation. No rearrangement of streets is contemplated or provided. The streets throughout Project Area B are exactly the same as are the streets in all parts of the District of Columbia. . . .

In sum the purpose of the plan, in addition to the elimination of slum conditions, is to create a pleasant neighborhood, in which people in well-balanced proportions as to income may live. The Government is to determine what conditions are pleasant, what constitutes the "most appropriate" pattern of land use, what is a good balance of income groups for a neighborhood, how many poor people, how many moderately well-to-do people, how many families of two, how

[59]

many of four, etc., should be provided for in this neighborhood, and what the proper development of a community should be.

Of course the plan as pictured in the prospectus is attractive. . . . If undertaken by private persons the project would be most laudable. . . . But as yet the courts have not come to call such pleasant accomplishments a public purpose. . . .[44]

The case was appealed to the Supreme Court of the United States. Mr. Justice Douglas, speaking for the Court, laid great stress upon the end envisioned by the D. C. Act—a more "beautiful. . .spacious. . .well-balanced" city and the elimination of slum property. Such an object, the opinion states, is within the general police powers of a state or the District of Columbia. "In such cases," the Court said, "the legislature, not the judiciary, is the main guardian of the public needs to be served by social legislation, whether it be Congress legislating concerning the District of Columbia. . .or the States legislating concerning local affairs." But what about the traditional constitutional protection of an individual against the seizure of his property for other than a public purpose? Seizure, the Court said, "is merely the means to the end" and "once the object is within the authority of Congress, the means by which it will be attained is also for Congress to determine."[45] And the Court continued:

. . . Here one of the means chosen is the use of private enterprise for redevelopment of the area. Appellants argue that this makes the project a taking from one businessman for the benefit of another businessman. But the means of executing the project are for Congress and Congress alone to determine, once the public purpose has been established.

After upholding the doctrine that the end justifies the means, the Court further stated:

We do not sit to determine whether a particular housing project is or is not desirable. The concept of the public welfare is broad and inclusive. . . . It is within the power of the legislature to determine that the community should be beautiful as well as healthy, spacious as well as clean, well-balanced as well as carefully patrolled. . . .

---

[44] 117 F. Supp. 705 (D.D.C. 1953). (Emphasis added.)

[45] 348 U.S. 26 (1954). Elsewhere the Court stated that "the role of the judiciary in determining whether that power [eminent domain] is being exercised for a public purpose is an extremely narrow one."

The fact that a property is "innocuous and unoffending" makes no difference, the Court held, and on the question of an individual owner's rights, the Court took the position that "if owner after owner were permitted to resist these redevelopment programs on the ground that his particular property was not being used... [for] the public interest, integrated plans for redevelopment would suffer greatly."[46]

And the Court concluded:

It is not for the courts to oversee the choice of the boundary line nor to sit in review on the size of a particular project area. Once the question of the public purpose has been decided, the amount and character of land to be taken for the project and the need for a particular tract to complete the integrated plan rests in the discretion of the legislative branch.

. . . If the Agency considers it necessary in carrying out the redevelopment project to take full title to the real property involved, it may do so. It is not for the courts to determine whether it is necessary for successful consummation of the project that unsafe, unsightly, or insanitary buildings alone be taken or whether title to the land be included, any more than it is the function of the courts to sort and choose among the various parcels selected for condemnation.

The Court's deference to the legislative will in this case provides an interesting contrast with its earlier view that—

. . . Government can scarcely be deemed free where the rights of property are left solely dependent upon the will of a legislative body without any restraint.[47]

Recalling William Pitt's statement that "the poorest man may in his cottage bid defiance to all the forces of the Crown" and that "the rain may enter, but the King of England cannot enter," Pro-

---

[46] It is of interest in this connection to contrast the limitations imposed by the Court upon its power to protect an individual against seizure of his property with its assertions of power to protect individual rights in other situations. The statement quoted above, as reported, reads ". . . on the ground that his particular property was not being used *against* the public interest. . . ." (Emphasis added.) Presumably, this was intended to read "for the public interest" instead of "against it."

[47] Wilkinson v. Leland 27 U.S. (2 Pet.) 627 (1829).

fessor Haar of the Harvard Law School observed recently that "the Supreme Court, by upholding in sweeping terms urban redevelopment legislation, has ruled in effect that the King not only may enter, but may remain, in the name of the general good, indeed for the very purpose of keeping the rain out."[48]

Is the Urban Renewal Program Anti-Constitutional?

The decision in *Berman* v. *Parker* illustrates a point made by the late Solicitor General James M. Beck. The Supreme Court, he wrote, has left the constitutionality of "general welfare" legislation largely up to Congress. In the case of urban renewal the Court holds, in effect, that the question of whether seizure of a particular piece of property is constitutional is not an appropriate question for judicial determination—that it is "non-justiciable." In other words, as Mr. Beck has pointed out, a statute may be "*anti*-constitutional," as a matter of fact although not declared "*un*constitutional," as a matter of law.[49] "This distinction," he noted, "while of great importance, is not easy to define and is most often ignored." Moreover, as Mr. Beck also pointed out, aside from questions which the Court leaves to political discretion, "many unconstitutional measures are passed and put into operation with no litigated case arising to invoke the judgment of the Court or arising too late to be an effective challenge."[50]

When the constitutionality of a proposed bill is questioned during congressional debate it is frequently argued, in effect, that the legislative branch need not be too concerned; that such matters are for the Supreme Court. But, as the late Mr. Beck has well said:

---

[48] Charles M. Haar, *Land-Use Planning: A Case Book on the Use, Misuse, and Re-use of Urban Land* (Boston: Little, Brown and Company, 1959), p. vii.

[49] ". . . a statute may be politically *anti*-constitutional without being juridically unconstitutional." James M. Beck and Merle Thorpe, *Neither Purse Nor Sword* (New York: The Macmillan Company, © 1936), p. 52. Quotations used by permission of the Macmillan Company.

[50] *Ibid.*

. . . This is a great illusion . . . the practice has steadily grown in Congress to regard discussions of constitutionality as academic by passing any kind of legislation and then leaving it to the Supreme Court. This might serve the purpose if every such law speedily reached the Court before damage were done. The fact is that few unconstitutional laws ever are reviewed by that tribunal. *Throughout our history there have been thousands of laws passed by the Congress and as many unauthorized executive acts for which the Constitution gave no sanction.* In the absence of a litigated case none of these was considered by the Supreme Court.[51]

Continuing, Mr. Beck wrote:

. . . The average citizen looks with indifference upon the measures passed by Congress and the acts of the executive because he suffers from the delusion that in every case the Court will prevent any violation of the Constitution and that government, as he understands it, will in some mysterious way go on as it has gone in the past. He has been lulled into a false sense of security and he has relaxed that "eternal vigilance" which is the price of liberty.[52]

. . . No constitution will last if its perpetuity depends solely upon the judiciary. There must be in the halls of Congress and in the executive offices a sense of constitutional morality.[53]

It must be acknowledged, of course, that as a legal matter "the Constitution means what the Supreme Court says it means,"[54] but the Court itself has pointed out in connection with its view of the general welfare clause that "there have been great statesmen in our history who have stood for other views."[55] In fact, the Court's view of the welfare clause is still debated among lawyers today. A recent article in the *American Bar Association Journal* (January 1961) examines the history of the general welfare clause and concludes that "there is no 'general welfare power' in the Constitution."[56] Citing the federal urban renewal program to illustrate the view that the welfare clause is misused, the article asserts that "the

---

[51] *Ibid.*, pp. 107-08. (Italics added.)

[52] *Ibid.*, p. 110.

[53] *Ibid.*, p. 107.

[54] Attributed to the late Chief Justice Hughes prior to his appointment to the Supreme Court.

[55] Helvering v. Davis, 301 U.S. 619, 640 (1937).

[56] George W. Nilsson, "There Is No 'General Welfare Power' in the Constitution of the United States," p. 43.

deterioration of cities is due to the failure of the cities to enforce their building and health regulations, and its correction is purely a local matter." In connection with a proposal to create a federal Department of Urban Affairs to deal with "such problems as inadequate housing, residential and industrial slums, double shift schools, inefficient mass transit systems, congested streets, water shortages and sewage disposal," the author concludes that—

> Every one of these problems is purely local. If the local communities are unable to take care of them, that tragic conclusion is an acknowledgement that the people are unable to govern themselves.[57]

---

[57] *Ibid.*, pp. 43-44.

CHAPTER V

Urban Renewal Programs

Federal Planning and Performance

LET US NOW turn to what has been taking place in urban renewal. Under the federal program, as of year-end 1959, 699 urban renewal project approvals, including 42 for general neighborhood renewal planning, were outstanding.[1] In addition, 28 demonstration projects were in execution (18) or completed (10), and 12 feasibility surveys were in the planning stage. Of the 699 approved projects, 309 were in the planning stage, 364 were in the execution stage, and 26 had been completed. Approved urban renewal projects were located in 417 localities; 269 of these projects were in localities with less than 50,000 population. Also nine of the 26 completed projects were in localities of less than 50,000 population (1950 census).

As of December 31, 1959, the Federal Government had authorized $1.7 billion in capital grant funds.[2] Some $1,388,647,765 of this had been reserved or earmarked for these 699 projects. Aggregate capital grant disbursements amounted to $233,294,000. Thus, more than $1.1 billion of committed funds was still to be disbursed.

The Urban Renewal Administration publication, *Urban Renewal Project Characteristics*, December 31, 1959, lists 437 projects as having reached advanced planning[3] or having received Urban Renewal Administration approval for project execution. In

---

[1] Unless otherwise noted, all data relative to the federal program are as of December 31, 1959, and are from HHFA, *Thirteenth Annual Report*, 1959 (Washington: Government Printing Office, n.d.), and from HHFA, *Urban Renewal Project Characteristics*, December 31, 1959. Detailed 1960 data were not available at the time of writing.

[2] Total authorization was raised to $4 billion by the Housing Act of 1961.

[3] Advanced planning means that a definite plan with delineation of the project area has been developed; execution means the plan is being carried out.

429 of these projects clearance data susceptible to analysis is provided. Eighty-six percent of these projects are reported as suffering from residential blight. A total of 235,173 existing dwelling units is shown, approximately 80 percent of which are said to be substandard. The report indicates that the 429 projects comprise a total of 22,362 gross acres which when completely redeveloped will yield 6,174 acres of public rights of way; 8,036 acres of commercial, industrial, and public land; and 8,152 acres of residential lands.

A majority of the reporting projects give estimates of proposed standard dwellings to be included upon completion. Proposed residential acreage is also shown. Analysis of these data indicate that an average of 18.6 dwelling units[4] per net acre in the finished projects may be expected. In many cases the density is as low as four per acre; in some, as high as 160. Applying the average to the total residential acres in the 429 projects we find an expected total of approximately 150,000 standard dwelling units[5] replacing 235,173 substandard and standard units.

This is not to say that 150,000 units have been built or rehabilitated. The report of the Federal Housing Administration of

---

[4] *Urban Renewal Project Characteristics, op. cit.*, shows (p. 9) 238 out of 429 projects report 136,739 proposed dwelling units, and that 8,152 acres of project land is classified as residential and public exclusive of rights of way. Having reference to the 429 projects as listed on pages 18 through 36, these data break down as follows:

Projects		Acres
133	all commercial or industrial	. . . .
238	reporting dwelling units	7,340
34	reporting public land without dwelling units	226
24	not reporting number of dwelling units	586
429 projects		8,152 acres

The average number of dwelling units per acre was determined by dividing 136,739 d.u.'s by 7,340 acres. The result, 18.6, was then multiplied by 586, the acreage of projects not reporting dwelling units. This result, 10,894, was added to the 136,739 units reported. The sum 147,633 was rounded off at an estimated 150,000 units planned for 262 projects.

[5] See footnote 4 above.

November 1, 1960 shows 18,730 rental units and 1,429 new and rehabilitated homes completed with FHA insured mortgage financing. To this total of 20,159 must be added approximately 5,000 more rental and cooperative units completed under conventional financing. Thus, literally hundreds of local governmental agencies supported by special legislation and liberal subsidy have been working together with a number of federal agencies for a period of ten years in an all-out attack on slums and the final result is, in round numbers, 25,000 new or rehabilitated dwelling units.[6]

If projects providing for 150,000 new and rehabilitated houses have been planned, the question arises as to why only 25,000 have been finished. It is true that private enterprise has been slow to show interest in this work and now generally only does so with FHA mortgage insurance guarantees. However, to get the answer we must know the meaning of the term "advanced planning and execution," used to describe the status of the 150,000 proposed units. "Advanced planning" is a description of the paper work and preliminary approvals whereas "execution" means the beginning of condemnation and demolition. The latter is naturally a slow process and properly should be so to assure property owners just recompense. "Execution" can drag on for many months before individual parcels of land are acquired, cleared, and assembled for offer to prospective purchasers. Thus at the time of the FHA report, only a minor portion of the residential acreage proposed for the 150,000 units was ready for consideration by redevelopers. With these facts in mind it would appear that private enterprise has kept pace with the program in a reasonably satisfactory manner.

---

[6] Senator Paul Douglas, in the course of Senate hearings on the urban renewal program, commented relative to the reported progress in construction of housing units in the midwestern region, in 1957: "So here we have almost a quarter of the population of the country and you mean to say that the program has been in effect for 8 years and at the end of it you point to 3,621 units developed. I would say the mountain labored and brought forth an exceedingly small mouse." U.S. Senate, Subcommittee of the Committee on Banking and Currency, *Hearings, Urban Renewal in Selected Cities*, 85th Congress, 1st Session, 1957, p. 59.

In nearly all cases to date the urban renewal process has started with consideration of blighted residential areas including a high percentage of substandard housing units. The finished area may be all residential or mixed residential, commercial, or industrial. In some cases it may be all commercial or industrial.

The substandard unit, predominating as it does in the primary consideration, appears to be a useful unit of measure when examining the cost of the total process. In the foregoing statistics we find 414 projects reporting 186,760 substandard and 47,230 standard dwelling units. The total net project cost before construction or rehabilitation is $1,315,016,000 or $7,041 per substandard unit.[7] The President's Advisory Committee on Government Housing Policies and Programs in its report of 1953 estimated that 6.8 million substandard dwelling units needed replacement or rehabilitation.[8] Applying the unit of measure, $7,041 per substandard dwelling unit, we find a total program costing the Federal and local governments $47,878,800,000 exclusive of the cost of new construction and rehabilitation.

Assuming that private industry will find the construction end worthwhile, let us take a look at the time element. We have seen from the foregoing statistics that 187,760 substandard units have been reported in 414 of 429 projects. The remaining 15 projects

----

[7] *Urban Renewal Project Characteristics, op. cit.,* p. 9, shows that 414 of 429 projects report 233,990 original dwelling units of which 186,760 were substandard. The tables on pages 12-13 show that the net project cost for 429 projects is estimated as $1,409,426,000. Having reference to pages 18-36 data appear for 12 projects with predominantly open land, 2 projects with open land, 12 projects classed as disaster areas, and 7 additional projects not reporting original dwelling units. Since the purpose of most of these projects was other than removal of substandard housing, their net project cost, $94,410,000, was deducted from the above total for 429 projects leaving $1,315,016,000. This was then divided by 186,760 substandard units to obtain the estimated cost, $7,041, per substandard unit. The total substandard units (186,760) includes some units chargeable against those projects for which the $94,410,000 was deducted. However these were left in the total for the sake of obtaining a more conservative estimated cost per unit.

[8] The President's Advisory Committee on Government Housing Policies and Programs, *A Report to the President of the United States* (Washington: Government Printing Office, December 1953).

reported a total of 1,183 dwellings without differentiating between standard and substandard. Counting all of these as substandard, we have a total of 188,943 substandard units for the 429 projects, which in a period of ten years have been brought into the advanced planning or execution stage. Granting that this is somewhat removed from the "brick and mortar stage," it would still be interesting to estimate the length of time necessary to move into advanced planning and execution on a front broad enough to assure ultimate elimination of our worst slums.

For this purpose we should recognize the inherent slowness of a new program and estimate that hereafter local public agencies and the Federal Government should move ahead much more rapidly. As an example, we will assume that progress in planning will quadruple the 188,943 substandard units referred to above. This means that we might optimistically look forward to development of urban renewal plans in the next ten years which would, in round numbers, assure the elimination of 750,000 substandard units. Going back to the recommendations and findings of former President Eisenhower's Advisory Committee, we recall the estimate of 6.8 million substandard units needing demolition or rehabilitation. Thus even at the stepped-up fourfold rate of production this gigantic task might still require as much as 90 years to complete.

A collateral program in the urban renewal process is that of relocating displaced persons. The need for such a program becomes apparent when we see in the foregoing statistical analysis that 235,173 original dwelling units dwindle to 150,000 in the finished projects. In addition the new standard dwelling units are generally far above the economic means of the original inhabitants of the area. These people are supposed to find residence in standard existing housing, public housing, or relocation housing constructed under FHA insured mortgages as provided for under section 221 of the National Housing Act. As of November 1, 1960, 19,904 homes and apartment units had been constructed with this federal assistance. Even these, in many instances, cannot be afforded by the relocatees.

Another phase of relocation is the problem presented by business concerns in the project areas. Federal aid up to $3,000 per case has been available to a business displaced by urban renewal to cover moving expenses and any direct losses of property, or, if greater, the total moving expenses may be allowed. Unfortunately there is no recompense provided for loss of good will or profit. However, the Housing Act of 1961 removes this limitation and authorizes low-interest government loans to businesses which suffer substantial economic injury as a result of displacement.[9]

The architectural characteristics of the new urban renewal housing runs the gamut. The current inventory includes individual detached homes, row houses, modern town houses, and walk-up and elevator high-rise apartments. Construction and design include the minimum permissible under local codes as well as luxury types with glass and aluminum exteriors and carpeted, air-conditioned interiors.

The costs of individual homes may range from $12,000 to $20,000. Rentals are from $17 to $45 per room. In general the projects have been financially successful although, in some cases, initial occupancy has presented a problem because of the proximity of remaining uncleared slums.

A few projects include a combination of low-rent public housing and minimum private-ownership housing, thus providing accommodations for the low-income groups which typically inhabit slum areas. However most of the projects are designed to accommodate occupants from higher income groups. In nearly all cases, it seems that the planning and construction have been good and represent a permanent improvement of the area.

MUNICIPAL RENEWAL EFFORTS

Many U.S. cities have undertaken to improve themselves by utilizing more fully their own local powers of government. Most of the municipal programs for urban renewal and upgrading of the housing inventory have centered around efforts to enforce housing codes. These efforts generally have been concentrated upon inspection and enforcement of minimum standards relative

---

[9] See "The Housing Act of 1961," p. 42.

to health and safety. In general, this has resulted in rehabilitation or demolition of housing unit structures which had become dilapidated or which lacked adequate plumbing, as well as the conservation of declining neighborhoods and individual structures not yet substandard in quality.

Baltimore, Maryland, has received wide publicity because of its plan for block-by-block inspection and its enforcement program which was coupled with a special housing court to expedite and facilitate action. Charlotte, North Carolina, began a vigorous code enforcement program in 1948, the results of which were so dramatic, in a city of low housing standards, that it was possible for Nash to report that "Charlotte's modest code provisions coupled with vigorous enforcement made permanent, visible improvements in its housing stock."[9] In 1958, *The Charlotte Observer* reported that well over 11,000 dwelling units had been brought up to standard quality, while almost 2,000 others had been demolished during the nearly ten years of operation of Charlotte's housing program.[10] Cincinnati, Ohio, also has had a special enforcement program which has been under the direction of a special housing division of the city government.

In St. Louis, Missouri, a single housing inspector was authorized to examine a dwelling for all types of code violations. The St. Louis program relied basically upon inspection to achieve results and its inspectors have reported that in many instances they were able to induce owners to make property improvements over and beyond those minimally required by city codes. Code enforcement in Rochester, New York, was aided by a public relations program which proved to be of great value in securing voluntary compliance to code standards. Los Angeles, California, not only established a comprehensive housing code with authority

---

[9] William W. Nash, *Residential Rehabilitation: Private Profits and Public Purposes* (New York: McGraw-Hill Book Company, Inc., 1959), p. 86. Nash describes in some detail many of the city enforcement programs herein referred to briefly. Details about several of these city programs also can be found in *Blueprint for Neighborhood Conservation* (Washington: National Association of Real Estate Boards, n.d.).

[10] February 26, 1958.

centralized in one department, but it also gave this department the power to repair or demolish structures whose owners refused to take the action necessary to bring them into compliance with the city code.

Pittsburgh, Pennsylvania's remarkable postwar accomplishments have been of interest to many other cities. A determined smoke control program is said to have reduced Pittsburgh's smoke by nearly 90 percent.[11] Gateway Center, a development financed by private funds, is a striking achievement, as is the rebuilding of Pittsburgh's Golden Triangle.

Indianapolis, Indiana, has a most unusual redevelopment program in that it was initiated locally and all of its funds are derived from local property tax levies and from bonds issued by the Redevelopment District. Both land clearance and redevelopment and rehabilitation are integral parts of the Indianapolis program. It is not associated with the federal grant-in-aid program, but is run entirely on a local basis. As of the end of 1959, some 190 acres had been redeveloped under the Indianapolis program, including provision of a new residential district, with its related community and shopping facilities, and a new commercial district.[12]

In Newark, New Jersey, in Kansas City, Missouri, in New Orleans, Louisiana, and in other cities throughout the Nation, municipal code enforcement has been undertaken in order to promote conservation of neighborhoods and to rehabilitate areas where blight and slum already have left their marks. Unfortunately, most cities in the United States either lack a housing code or they are not rigorously enforcing their codes.[13] In those cities which established *and enforced* effective housing codes, the beneficial effects upon their housing inventories have been substantial. Even though municipal code enforcement probably has never been fully utilized anywhere in the United States, it nevertheless

---

[11] Arthur B. Van Buskirk, "What Business Has Learned About Rebuilding a City," *The "Little" Economies* (New York: Committee for Economic Development, 1958), p. 25.

[12] *Progress Report* (Indianapolis: Indianapolis Redevelopment Commission, n.d.), esp. pp. 3-4, 13, 15.

[13] Nash, *op. cit.*, p. 85.

has been responsible, in the aggregate, for raising many thousands of dwelling units from substandard to standard quality.

PRIVATE RENEWAL EFFORTS

Recent interest in the programs and expeditures contemplated under the federal urban renewal program has tended to obscure the activities and opportunities of municipal programs as well as the possibilities for urban renewal through enterpreneurial efforts. Also, of course, the custom of presenting the federal program in aggregate terms makes the federal program appear more striking when placed alongside individual municipal and private activities.

Mr. Peter Turchon has been widely publicized because of his longstanding work in rehabilitating older houses. Nash quoted the *Boston Sunday Herald* as describing Turchon as "America's one-man urban program." Mr. Turchon is in business and makes a profit from his activities. At the same time he has been responsible for rehabilitating thousands of run-down dwelling units during his years of operation. He was reported to be remodeling at an annual rate of 500 structures "long before 1957."[14]

Among other illustrations of entrepreneurial activity, Nash also describes the rehabilitation work of Mr. John F. Havens in Columbus, Ohio. Havens entered the rehabilitation business in 1951 and by early 1957 had sold or rented some 500 rehabilitated dwelling units.[15] The typical selling price for a house he had remodeled was $8,000, the typical rental, $60 a month.[16]

Havens' activities are of particular interest because he provided housing in modest neighborhoods to families whose average annual *family* income ranged from $3,000 to $4,000.[17]

These are several illustrations of the activities carried on all over the Nation by local entrepreneurs who, motivated by the search for profits, are doing much to provide better housing for thousands of persons. In many instances, such rehabilitation may be a very small-scale operation in which an individual purchases

[14] *Ibid.*, pp. 62-70.
[15] *Ibid.*, p. 71.
[16] *Ibid.*
[17] *Ibid.*

a run-down house, does much of the physical work of rehabilitation himself, and then subsequently resells it.

Various "prestige" rehabilitation developments have taken place too, such as the well-known Georgetown area in Washington, D.C., and the perhaps almost equally well-known revitalization of the Near North Side in Chicago, Illinois. While comebacks of declining neighborhoods such as those of Chicago's Near North Side and Washington's Georgetown certainly are interesting and important, their prestige character makes them somewhat exceptional.

Of considerable interest also is the widely publicized work of Chicago's Back of the Yards Council. The area back of the stockyards in Chicago is a long-established community of rather modest homes in which thousands of persons live. The Back of the Yards Council encouraged the city government to enforce building codes and zoning and sanitation laws in the area. Social pressure was employed to induce owners to repair their homes. A program of new home building was begun, with financing facilitated through savings and loan associations in the area. Titles on vacant lots were cleared, new homes have been built, and vacant commercial stores have been converted, when feasible, to residential apartments.[18] The area back of the Chicago stockyards has been improved as a result of the combined efforts of this nonprofit organization and the residents of the area.

In various cities, real estate boards, chambers of commerce, and other local groups have sparked drives to improve their cities through the enactment and enforcement of realistic housing codes and through appeals to personal and civic pride and interest. The aggregate effect has been to improve the housing and general community conditions of uncounted thousands of citizens. In 1958, it was stated that over 4,000 homes in the back of the yards section alone of Chicago had "undergone *major* repair and remodeling work."[19] The nationwide possibilities for improving our housing

---

[18] See *Housing Act of 1958, Hearings,* U. S. House of Representatives, Subcommittee on Housing, Committee on Banking and Currency, 85th Congress, 2d Session, July 7-11, 14-18, 1958, esp. pp. 579-84.
[19] *Ibid.,* p. 581 (Italics added.)

inventory by effective action of this kind seem enormous. The local renewal activities mentioned above do not constitute an exhaustive presentation of such activities; they are simply illustrative of some of the potential for accomplishment through local renewal activities.

Another indicator of what is being done is the activity in the FHA Home Improvement Program. Unlike other federal programs discussed herein this is not dependent upon federal planning or control. Homeowners can get loans from banks, savings and loan associations, and other lenders approved by FHA. The homeowner contacts the lender direct or through dealer contractors without the necessity of Federal Housing Administration prior approval or supervision of the work. The maximum home improvement loan is $3,500 and the term of the loan is up to five years. The favorable terms and convenience afforded the borrower result from FHA insurance of the lender's portfolio of improvement loans.

FHA reports the typical loan as being just under $1,000. It is most frequently for additions and alterations. Other types of work generally financed under this plan include insulation, heating, plumbing, roofing, and painting and decorating. This business has grown to an annual volume of one million loans which total over $1 billion.

CHAPTER VI

Costs of Urban Renewal

Costs of the Urban Renewal Process

IN MOST ANY way that one chooses to view the costs of urban renewal, they constitute vast amounts in the aggregate. The several hundreds of billions of dollars of wealth in the United States are located largely in the cities, and a major proportion of this wealth is in the form of residential structures.[1] The Committee for Economic Development states that the value of tangible real estate in the cities is more than $500 billion.[2] Professor Colin Clark states that "in most countries the order of magnitude of the stock of residential capital is equal to about one year's national product."[3]

Every individual householder, including the renter, is keenly aware of the costs of maintaining his investment in household goods. The homeowner is particularly conscious of the annual costs he incurs for general maintenance, for repairs, and for renovation and upgrading, whether the latter is to install a shower, a water closet, or central air conditioning. And some householders are confronted with costs resulting from the changing character of neighborhoods, moves from one housing unit to another, and the like.

Urban renewal costs, private and governmental, are of great magnitude. Physical deterioration, obsolescence, and changing use-requirements affect all the components of cities. Structures

---

[1] Edward C. Banfield and Morton Grodzins, *Government and Housing in Metropolitan Areas* (New York: McGraw-Hill Book Company, Inc., 1958), "Foreword," p. x.

[2] Research and Policy Committee of the Committee for Economic Development and of the Area Development Committee, *Guiding Metropolitan Growth* (New York: Committee for Economic Development, August 1960), p. 7.

[3] Colin Clark, *Growthmanship*, Hobart Paper No. 10 (London: Institute of Economic Affairs, 1961).

of all kinds require continual maintenance, eventual demolition, and, in many instances, replacement. Other structures must be upgraded, converted to different uses, or demolished when their usefulness has been outlived. In order best to serve the public, standard quality houses may be razed to permit the construction of a shopping center—a land-use change. And, even though this will maximize total satisfaction or returns from resources, such changes are effected only at a cost. The maintenance, modernization, and replacement costs of public facilities such as streets, bridges, schools, sewers, and the like are substantial and continuing. The sheer magnitude of the real wealth of the cities, coupled with the costs attendant upon needs arising from physical deterioration, obsolescence, and the reallocation of resources, assures the cities of large annual renewal costs at all times.

Costs of the Federal Urban Renewal Program

Estimates of the costs of the federal urban renewal program vary substantially, although all such estimates envision the outlay of a great deal of money. Many of the estimates do not undertake a rigorous distinction among expenditures made by federal, state, and local governments, and by private parties. The proportion of total costs incurred by various groups will be affected by the nature and execution of urban renewal program activities and by governmental policies relative to degree of subsidization.

The Subcommittee on Urban Redevelopment of the President's Advisory Committee on Government Housing Policies and Programs estimated conservatively, in 1953, that $1.5 billion would have to be budgeted annually for a period of ten years (a total of $15 billion) as the federal and local contribution *for slum clearance alone.*[4] This figure represents the cost to place cleared land in the hands of builders who will construct new dwelling units. It was based on the estimated need for immediate treatment of 6,800,000 substandard dwellings 5,000,000 of which would have to be demolished and 1,800,000 of which could be rehabilitated. The cost of redevelopment projects needed to accomplish this

---

[4] *A Report to the President . . ., op. cit.,* p. 111.

work was established by assuming that federal and local cost would average $3,000 per unit to be demolished. In Chapter V, it was seen that reappraisal of such a program in the light of recent data indicates a probable cost of over $47 billion to local and federal government. Projection of this kind of estimate to include construction costs of new building improvements and rehabilitation of existing structures may result in a total cost of $100 billion or more.

Two government officials and a university professor joined together to estimate urban renewal program costs for inclusion in a major study published by The Twentieth Century Fund. Their 1955 estimate was that, at 1950 prices, urban renewal activities would cost from $85.5-$91.3 billion, where emphasis was primarily upon housing and related facilities.[5] These estimates were for a limited program only, that of redeveloping residential neighborhoods. The authors (Bloomberg, *et al*) said that much more should be done, citing the following as being needed: high-speed traffic arteries, bridges, tunnels, public rapid transit, interurban terminals, airports, public administration buildings, schools, hospitals, recreation centers, face-lifting of Main Street, elimination of smoke, noise, and odors. As they point out, data are not available either for estimating the costs of all of these proposed activities or even for determining what should be undertaken and what it would cost.[6] The Committee for Economic Development recently (1960) adjusted these figures for changes in construction costs and computed that the current cost would be $120-$125 billion.[7] CED also stated in its report:

> Estimates of the capital requirements to renew our cities cover a wide range—from 120 billion dollars up. These estimates assume that three-fourths to seven-eights of the total outlay will take the form of private capital outlay.[8]

[5] Lawrence H. Bloomberg, Howard G. Brunsman, and A. Benjamin Handler, "Urban Redevelopment," in J. Frederic Dewhurst and Associates, *America's Needs and Resources, A New Survey* (New York: The Twentieth Century Fund, 1955), p. 512; see esp. pp. 509-12 for a discussion of size of the program and its cost.

[6] *Ibid.*

[7] *Guiding Metropolitan Growth, op. cit.*, note 3, p. 36.

[8] *Ibid.*, p. 7.

A special study panel for the Rockefeller Brothers Fund reported in 1958:

> The investment required to make our cities attractive and healthy places in which to live has been estimated as running into the hundreds of billion dollars.[9]

The following colloquy between Representative Albert Thomas, Chairman of the House Subcommittee responsible for urban renewal appropriations, former Federal Housing Commissioner Norman P. Mason, and the then Commissioner of Urban Renewal, Richard L. Steiner, further illustrates the magnitude and continuing nature of the program:

MR. THOMAS. . . . Your grant money is $1,300 million in round figures. We are getting up into some money here.

What do you think you will spend in the next 10 years? How long will it be before you get 90 percent of the program behind you? By the time you do that you have to rub it out and start all over again, do you not?

MR. MASON. The Committee on Economic Development has done some guessing on this, and they have a constantly increasing figure in their estimate.

MR. THOMAS. Have you people done any figuring on it?

MR. STEINER. I do not think there is any really good, reliable figure of the total national need.[10]

The evidence seems ample that costs of urban renewal programs involve very high aggregate figures. It is also important to note, however, the open-end character of the typical urban renewal cost estimate. The above-cited estimates (The Twentieth Century Fund study, The Committee For Economic Development study, and The Rockefeller Brothers Fund report) are typical of cost estimates of urban renewal programmed activities. The urban renewal programs discussed therein lack objective delineation. If there are finite limits to the envisioned programs, the limits are

---

[9] Report of Panel IV of the Special Studies Project, *The Challenge to America: Its Economic and Social Aspects* (Garden City: Doubleday & Company, Inc., 1958), p. 45. Quoted by permission of Doubleday & Company, Inc.

[10] Hearings before the Subcommittee on Independent Offices of the House Committee on Appropriations, 1959, pp. 827-28.

not clearly drawn. Consequently, even these estimates may well prove to be far below the actual costs which would be incurred if the proposed programs were executed.

Why Costs Are High

The preceding discussion already has indicated, at least implicitly, some of the reasons why estimates of aggregate urban renewal costs involve such staggering sums. The very nature of the urban renewal process, coupled with the enormous investments in our cities, means that annual costs of urban renewal will be very large. All of the components of the cities require regular maintenance and repair. Many must be converted from one use to another in response to changed needs. Both physical deterioration and obsolescence eventually make demolition necessary. Replacement of worn-out facilities, if they are still wanted, must be undertaken. And, finally, because of changing demand and supply (cost) conditions, resources must be reallocated as to uses.

In any large city the performance of these functions will require the expenditure of many millions of dollars each year by homeowners, by residential landlords, by owners of commercial and industrial properties, by school districts, by municipal departments, and by other property owners. Where billions of dollars in investments are involved, the aggregate costs are substantial for necessary maintenance, repairs, renovation, demolition, changing uses, and desired replacement of demolished structures.

It is commonly pointed out that cities, like Topsy, have just grown and that, as a result, many incompatible land uses and activity conjunctions have developed. Correcting incompatible uses and activities can be costly. This point has been elaborated frequently. Of far greater significance is the often-cited fact that urban renewal costs have reached staggering proportions because of the past, as well as the continuing, failure of many cities to renew themselves from year to year. Mayor Richard Daley of Chicago has pointed out that the enormous urban renewal task now confronting us did not arise overnight, but instead represents 50 or even 200 years of delay by the cities.[11]

Extended neglect by the cities has caused blight to develop and spread, slums to be created and vast areas of many cities to fall into a state of decay. In short, the failure of cities to renew themselves on a continuing basis has caused them to accumulate large quantities of worn-out and out-moded structures and facilities. In a sense, cities have been living on their capital. The present estimates of urban renewal costs reflect this by taking into consideration the need to eliminate the vast accumulations of worn-out components of the cities. These are costs which have been postponed, their postponement made possible partly by the durable character of so many of the structures and facilities within the cities.

The scope of urban renewal programs is a major factor in their great cost. Slum clearance, subsidized low-rent housing, rehabilitation of blighted areas, beautifying and face-lifting the cities all are costly. The attempt to revitalize parts of cities and even whole cities may require large expenditures if the efforts are directed to reversing the ebb tide of change. That is, if social and economic forces are operating so as to effect the decline of an area within a city or even of the city itself, it may be that these forces can be offset only through the outlay of substantial sums. Thus a New England city, largely dependent upon textile manufacturing, may be declining as the economic advantages it once enjoyed slip away because of changes in costs and availability of labor, transportation, and power resources. Revitalizing such a city might require great expenditures. In so far as urban renewal programs embrace such things as new airports, new public transit terminals, new schools, hospitals, and recreation centers, as envisioned in The Twentieth Century Fund study referred to earlier, their costs will be magnified yet more. Indeed, as those authors pointed out, we have no way of knowing how much such programs might

---

[11] U.S. House of Representatives, Subcommittee on Housing, Committee on Banking and Currency, *Hearings, Housing Act of 1959*, 86th Congress, 1st Session, January 28-31, February 2-3, 1959, p. 431.

cost.[12] The open-end character of most proposals for urban renewal programs establishes open-end cost estimates.

Costs of upgrading in response to changing standards can have tremendous impact upon the costs of proposed urban renewal plans. The problems of minimum and maximum housing standards and of zoning have been analyzed by Professors Banfield and Grodzins for the American Council to Improve Our Neighborhoods (ACTION).[13] Although Banfield and Grodzins advocate minimum zoning and housing regulations "to protect the health or safety of the community or to safeguard it against unreasonable social costs," they point out that often such standards are not in fact minimal in relationship to the foregoing needs, but instead often tend to reflect the tastes and preferences of others. They observed succinctly:

> To require the consumer to buy more housing or related facilities than he wants is both an infringement of his liberty and a malallocation of resources. There is no need to explain why it is the former. It is the latter because only the consumer is in a position to know what combination of goods and services—trees and sidewalks as against food and clothing, for example—will give him the greatest total satisfaction. Area-wide standards for building should not exceed genuine minimum standards. Definitions of "minimum" or "essential" should not be confused with definitions of "desirable" or even with exaggerated middle-class ideas of "adequate."[14]

Certainly, without engaging the merits of any particular item of housing standards, we can acknowledge that requiring higher-cost standards will have the same effect of raising urban renewal costs if urban renewal includes a program to raise all housing units to given standards. To illustrate, the Bureau of the Census has classified housing units as to quality. Units which meet certain criteria—nondilapidated, installed private tub or shower, installed private water closet, and hot and cold running water—are regarded as standard quality units. Units which do not meet all of these criteria are considered to be of substandard quality. It was in the 1950 Census that the criterion of hot running water

---

[12] Bloomberg, Brunsman, and Handler, *op. cit.*, p. 512.
[13] Banfield and Grodzins, *op. cit.*, esp. pp. 77-84.
[14] *Ibid.*, p. 78, and pp. 77-84, *passim.*

was introduced as an indicator of quality.[15] This had the effect of placing 1.4 million dwelling units, 3.2 percent of the 44.5 million units reporting condition and facilities, in the substandard housing category.[16] These 1.4 million units, if the criterion of hot running water had not been imposed, would otherwise have been regarded as standard quality dwelling units. Again, not engaging the merits of imposing the specific criterion, several facts are evident. Some consumers may prefer other things to the facility of hot running water. Further, the raising or adding to the criteria of "standard quality housing" obviously can be accomplished far more easily than the housing itself can be changed to meet the new minimal standards. And finally, each rise in, or addition to, the criteria of standard quality housing can add to the costs of urban renewal plans which are oriented largely towards housing programs.

Recently, weight has been given to beautifying and revitalizing the downtown sections of our great cities. The editors of *Fortune* magazine provide both a description and an evaluation of these planned city projects:

> . . . They will be spacious, parklike, and uncrowded. They will feature long green vistas. They will be stable and symmetrical and orderly. They will be clean, impressive, and monumental. They will have all the attributes of a well-kept, dignified cemetery.[17]

And further:

> These projects will not revitalize downtown; they will deaden it. For they work at cross-purposes to the city. They banish the street. They banish its function. They banish its variety.[18]

Yet these great projects which the editors of *Fortune* have described so eloquently, and denounced so vigorously as unworkable, do add greatly to the costs of many urban renewal programs. It is a costly venture to acquire large tracts of land in a city, raze the existing structures, tear out streets and sewers and other service facilities, and then establish sweeping malls, erect high-rise build-

---

[15] *Census of Housing: 1950, op. cit.*, p. XXXII.
[16] *Ibid.*, Table 7.
[17] *The Exploding Metropolis* (New York: Doubleday & Company, Inc., 1958), p. 157.
[18] *Ibid.*, pp. 157-58.

ings, and provide all the needed new service facilities. Beautifying the cities by what has sometimes been called "the bulldozer approach" is expensive by the very nature of the methods employed.

Slum clearance programs also have had their costs increased by the "bulldozer approach" to urban renewal. Mr. John P. McCollum, Regional Administrator, Region IV, of the Housing and Home Finance Agency, in 1957 introduced into the record of Senate hearings, relative to urban renewal and other housing problems, exhibits describing urban renewal projects in Chicago.[19] One of these exhibits briefly described 20 Chicago urban renewal projects. An examination of the exhibit shows that 17 of the 20 projects involved outright clearance of the structures then standing.[20] Of the other three projects, one involved land assembly and the other two a combination of rehabilitation and clearance.

Of considerable interest in explaining the high cost of the bulldozer approach in these projects was the fact that clearance frequently included the demolition of housing unit structures which were of standard quality. Among the 17 individual projects in which clearance was the treatment applied, standard quality housing units demolished, as a percent of the total units demolished in a given project, ranged from a low of 2.9 percent in one project to a high of 50.2 percent in another project. Considering the 17 projects as a whole, a total of 13,975 units were removed and, of these, 3,470 units were standard quality units.[21] Some 12,354 families were displaced. Thus, in these 17 projects, 24.8 percent of the units removed under the clearance program were standard quality housing units. (Mr. Phil A. Doyle, Executive Director of the Chicago Land Clearance Commission, advised that it costs about $120,000 per acre to purchase and clear land on Chicago's South Side.)[22]

The destruction of structurally sound, standard quality housing units adds substantially to the costs of an urban renewal program.

---

[19] *Urban Renewal in Selected Cities, Hearings,* 1957, *op. cit.,* pp. 67-81.
[20] *Ibid.,* pp. 72-80.
[21] HHFA Exhibits, *op. cit.,* pp. 72-80.
[22] *Ibid.,* pp. 49-50.

This is not to suggest or imply that the Chicago program is subject to any special criticism. The very nature of the bulldozer clearance approach leads to much the same problem in other cities as well. Former Housing Administrator Norman P. Mason pointed up this problem sharply, saying:

> Urban renewal is in danger of being thought of simply as a process of tearing down—but that's the least part of it. Most of our housing, most of our cities are basically sound, and our first responsibility is to keep it that way.[23]

The long-run costs of urban renewal programs have been pushed upwards in part because of the way in which the programs have been executed. As pointed out above, the "bulldozer" large-scale clearance approach had the effect of displacing large numbers of families from their homes. Mayor Anthony Celebreeze of Cleveland stated in hearings on the Housing Act of 1959 that people are taken out of one slum area and then crowded into another area which they then turn into a slum area also.[24] Alexander Summer, a member of the President's Advisory Committee on Housing Policies and Programs, has stated the same problem:

> . . . under the 1949 act, as fast as slums were cleared, it was necessary to cause people to move out of those slums, and as fast as they were cleared, new slums were created, in another part of the city, and where you cleared an area, oftentimes the use of the property thereafter had fewer families in it, less density, than the original section.
>
> So that, in clearing one slum, and spending millions and sometimes hundreds of millions of dollars, you have only moved the slums to other areas. . . .[25]

In short, the large-scale clearance approach in urban renewal has meant that urban renewal activities, in execution, have worked in many cases against themselves, often subverting the objectives of the program. New slums have been created as rapidly as old

---

[23] HHFA-OA-No. 60-155, News Release of March 15, 1960, p. 1.

[24] U.S. Senate, Committee on Banking and Currency, *Hearings, Housing Act of 1959*, 86th Congress, 1st Session, 1959.

[25] U.S. House of Representatives, Committee on Banking and Currency, *Hearings, Housing Act of 1954*, 83d Congress, 2d Session, 1954, p. 742.

ones have been eliminated. Some observers have described the process as that of chasing the slums around town. Not only are such activities ineffectual in coping with the problems of urban renewal but they also are manifestly costly.

Additionally, it has been recognized that the widespread municipal failure to cope with the causes of slums, as distinct from their symptoms, has been a basic weakness of formal urban renewal programs and thereby has contributed to the rapid formation of new slums. The Subcommittee on Urban Redevelopment of the President's Advisory Committee on Government Housing Policies and Programs included in its report the following highly significant statement.

Slums do not just happen. They are the product of neglect—neglect by landlords, by tenants, and by all of us who make up the communities in which slums exist. But above all else, they are the product of neglect by our city governments.

Although the importance of comprehensive city planning to orderly urban growth is well established, most cities fail to plan effectively.

Although zoning well framed and consistently enforced is widely accepted as essential to a stable city, many cities fail to enforce their zoning laws.

Although the overcrowding of dwellings long has been identified as the first and fundamental cause of slums, few cities enforce occupancy controls even in those areas not yet overcrowded but threatened with the next advance of blight.

Although building, fire, housing, and health codes exist in nearly all cities to prevent the growth of unsafe and unsanitary conditions, few, if any, cities attempt to enforce them.

Although parks and recreation areas are essential to the maintenance of healthy neighborhoods and are provided for that purpose in newer areas, few cities bother to provide them in the older crowded areas where the need is greatest.

Although street, alley, and sidewalk maintenance, street lighting, garbage collection, street cleaning, and other elementary phases of municipal housekeeping are known to be vital to neighborhood pride and spirit, few cities give anything but second-class attention to these responsibilities in older areas.

Although the confinement of any expanding group of people to a tightly congested part of a city must result in the over-crowding and exploitation which breeds slums, few, if any, cities have accepted responsibility for the segregation of minority racial groups into spaces so limited that they must of necessity become blighted.

These are some of the causes of slums. Their combined pressure pushes American cities along the deterioration pipeline faster than slums can be removed at one end and new dwellings added at the other.[26]

Frazar B. Wilde speaks of "the failure of cities and towns to prevent and mitigate slum areas by the means within their own control. The flagrant disregard of health rules, safety rules, construction rules, etc., by practically all major cities is well known and a grave reflection on our democratic process."[27]

The failure of city governments to cope with the *causes* of slums adds enormously to the costs of urban renewal. The unchecked spread of blight and slum formation erodes the values of the city at rapid rates raising the costs of urban renewal programs.

Another major cause of the high costs of urban renewal programs is the practice of paying inflated prices for slum properties. As a matter both of equity and of law, it is customary to consider the earnings from property in determining its valuation for condemnation purposes. Since the value of any resource is the capitalized value of its earnings, this is a sound basis for setting the price paid to the owner of seized property. Slum properties present some special problems of valuation however. Rental prices in slum areas frequently are remarkably high.

An Assistant Attorney General in New York recently reported a family was paying $143 monthly rent for a seven-room tenement which lacked even cooking facilities. An affidavit prepared by the Attorney General stated of one building that the landlord derived almost $3,500 per year in rent from it, although the building itself did not appear to have a sale value equal to that amount. (An interesting sidelight was the statement that this rent was "paid by the Department of Welfare of the City of New

---

[26] *A Report to the President, . . . op cit.*, pp. 108-09.
[27] Quoted in *Guiding Metropolitan Growth, op. cit.*, p. 39.

York. . . .") The State charged also that this building was characterized by fire hazards, a water-filled cellar, rotting floors and woodwork, peeling paint, vermin infestation, and a noxious stench.[28]

The Village President of Maywood, Illinois, stated that in a study of 534 families who are to be relocated from a project there, 13 percent of the families then renting were paying monthly rentals in excess of $100 for substandard housing.[29] Representatives of Rockford, Illinois, described dilapidated trailers, purchased from the Federal Government for prices ranging from $15 to $30 per trailer, which were being rented for $80 per month.[30] The high rentals in slum areas are familiar phenomena.

Landlords of slum properties frequently derive huge returns on their slum property investments. These inflated returns commonly are achieved through a violation of both moral standards and legal restrictions relative to housing: housing codes, fire codes, plumbing and sanitation codes, and so on. Capitalizing the improper or illegal earnings on these slum dwellings establishes a high valuation for slum properties.[31]

The value-inflating effect of capitalizing high earnings can be shown by a simple illustration. Assume that rental property earning $400 per annum is purchased for $8,000. A 5 percent return currently is being earned. Through illegal conversion and disregard of occupancy codes, the number of persons occupying the property is then greatly increased and earnings on the property rise to $1,600 per annum. If 5 percent per annum is assumed to be a "fair rate of return" for seizure valuation purposes, the capitalized value of the property's earnings will be $32,000—a fourfold increase over its original purchase price.

---

[28] *The New York Times*, August 5, 1960.

[29] Statement of John G. Trumbull, *Hearings, Urban Renewal in Selected Cities*, 1957, *op. cit.*, p. 183.

[30] Statement of Mayor Ben T. Schleicher, *et al.*, *Ibid.*, pp. 193-95.

[31] See Statements of Mayor Frank P. Zeidler of Milwaukee, Wisconsin, and of City Manager Julian H. Orr of Portland, Maine, *Ibid.*, pp. 173-74, 275-77; also Statement of Alexander Summer of President's Advisory Committee on Housing, *Hearings, Housing Act of 1954*, *op. cit.*, p. 741.

Nor is this farfetched. The Comptroller General of the United States reviewed slum clearance and urban renewal activities in San Francisco. A pertinent section of the Comptroller General's report stated:

The Corporation "dummy" acquired the property in 1952 at a price of $8,810, and shortly thereafter the "dummy" mortgaged the property to the previously referred to savings and loan association for $7,500. During 1955, the property was sold to the corporation for $15,000. The first real estate appraisal for acquisition by the LPA was made about the same time. The value established by the appraisal was $12,000. In arriving at this value, the appraiser considered net income from the structure which he estimated at $1,435 a year.

A second appraisal made in 1957 set a value of $21,700, and this value was based on comparable sales of similar property and estimated reproduction cost less depreciation. By that time, net rental income had increased to $4,742 a year, according to a schedule which the appraiser claimed was furnished by an officer of the corporation. In January 1958, the HHFA Regional Office authorized the LPA to acquire the property at a price not to exceed $21,750. The LPA then attempted to negotiate the purchase of the property but was unsuccessful because it refused to pay the corporation's asking price of $27,500. As were other corporation property cases, this case was referred to the court for decision.[32]

The Comptroller General reported in his findings:

Inflated prices are being paid for certain residential slum properties which were overvalued because rental income was collected by the owners on unlawfully occupied housing. The Federal Government generally pays two thirds of the cost of the slum clearance and urban renewal program and thus bears a large part of the excessive cost of acquiring slum dwellings.[33]

This report also stated that the Commissioner of the Urban Renewal Administration indicated that the effective long-range

---

[32] The Comptroller General of the United States, *Report to the Congress of the United States: Review of Slum Clearance and Urban Renewal Activities of the San Francisco Regional Office, Housing and Home Finance Agency, October 1959* (Washington: General Accounting Office, July 1960), p. 15.

[33] *Ibid.*, p. 5.

solution to the problem of overpayments for slum properties depends upon adequate local codes—zoning, housing, and construction—with rigid enforcement of those codes.[34] The Comptroller General's report further pointed out that the practice of paying inflated prices for slum properties was not confined to San Francisco, but instead characterized urban renewal projects in other cities as well.[35] In addition to this cost-incurring abuse, the report cited various other practices which have involved excessive or unwarranted costs for the urban renewal program.[36]

The Federal Government pays its two-thirds share of the net project cost by making a capital grant to the local renewal organization or local public agency (LPA).[37] The community pays its one-third share in cash or non-cash grants. Illustrative non-cash grants-in-aid are: (a) donations of land within the project area; (b) costs of installing, constructing, or reconstructing streets, utilities, and other site improvements; and (c) costs of providing public buildings and facilities such as parks, schools, recreation facilities, health centers, and various other installations.

The first two examples must be located inside the project area and be essential to its execution in order to qualify as local grants-in-aid. Facilities such as those in the third category qualify as non-cash grants-in-aid if they are of direct and substantial bene-

---

[34] *Ibid.*, p. 18.

[35] *Ibid.*, p. 12. Also in commenting upon the President's housing message in connection with the 1961 Housing Act, the editors of *House* & *Home* magazine addressed an open letter to the President pointing out: "And if, as you say, we need a broader and more effective program to remove blight, your plan to spend another $2.5 billion to buy up slums at prices three and four times their reuse value would not go very far. New York City alone might need every cent of that money to reclaim its 7,000 acres of blight and decay, for New York slum prices are so inflated by overcrowding and undertaxation that redevelopment purchases have averaged $481,000 an acre." *Congressional Record*, April 11, 1961, p. A2391.

[36] *Ibid.*, *passim.*

[37] A description of the provisions and operation of federal urban renewal legislation is presented in Chapter III.

fit to the project and are necessary to the ultimate redevelopment plan. If the facilities are of direct and substantial benefit to other areas as well, part of the cost may be allocated to the urban renewal project as a local grant-in-aid. Briefly, if the benefit to the project area is less than 10 percent, none of the cost is allocable as a local grant-in-aid; if the benefit exceeds 80 percent, the full cost is allocable to the project as a local grant-in-aid; if the project area receives 10-80 percent of the direct benefits of the facilities, the amount of the cost allocable as a local grant-in-aid depends upon the proportion of total benefits received by the project area.

Since many communities rely heavily upon non-cash grants-in-aid to pay their one-third share of net project cost (these non-cash items already have been included in gross project costs), the Federal Government, in many instances, pays two-thirds of the costs of the non-cash local grants-in-aid.

Table VII on page 92 illustrates the effect of non-cash grants by localities on the amount of the federal grant which is provided. In this example, the non-cash items increase project costs upon which the federal grant is based and reduce cash requirements upon the locality. A 100 percent allowance for public facilities raised net project cost by a third and this same allowance toward the one-third share of net cost to be contributed by the locality resulted in a one-third increase in the federal cash grant. The full allowance for non-cash local items meant that the Federal Government put up eight dollars in cash for each dollar the locality contributed. Where there was no allowance for local non-cash items the project cost was less, the federal grant was less, and the locality contributed one dollar in cash for each two dollars of federal grant.

From this illustration, given by the Comptroller General, it will be noted that the allowance made for public facilities as a local grant-in-aid is a major factor in determining the amount of the federal grant as well as how much cash the community or locality must contribute. Determination of a locality's grant-in-aid credit may raise materially the costs to the Federal Government of the urban renewal program. As the Comptroller General's Report made clear, transactions of this nature are not un-

Table VII

Alternate Assumptions as to Allowances Made for Local Grants-In-Aid

	100 percent allowance	50 percent allowance	No allowance
Cost of planning, acquiring land, relocating tenants, demolishing buildings	$12,000 [100% of cost]	$12,000 [100% of cost]	$12,000 [100% of cost]
Public facilities allowed as noncash local grants-in-aid (such as streets, sidewalks, sewers, schools, libraries, police and fire stations)	3,000 [100% of cost]	1,500 [50% of cost]	---- [no cost allowance]
Gross project cost	$15,000	$13,500	$12,000
Sale price of land	3,000	3,000	3,000
Net project cost	$12,000	$10,500	$9,000
Local share, one-third of net project cost:			
Cash grants-in-aid	$1,000	$2,000	$3,000
Noncash grants-in-aid	3,000	1,500	-----
	$4,000	$3,500	$3,000
Federal share, two-thirds of net project cost	8,000	7,000	6,000
	$12,000	$10,500	$9,000

Source: The Comptroller General of the United States, *Report to the Congress of the United States: Review of Slum Clearance and Urban Renewal Activities of the San Francisco Regional Office, Housing and Home Finance Agency, October 1959*, (Washington: General Accounting Office, July 1960), p. 22.

common.[38] Other earlier reports by the Comptroller General indicate that cost incurring practices are not isolated occurrences.[39]

Some observers feel that the process of urban renewal has been delayed by a tendency to allow the activities of *planning* urban renewal to supersede the urban renewal activities themselves. Various advocates of effective city code enforcement have noted that if effective enforcement had begun even as late as 1950, rather than devoting so much attention to discussions of urban renewal, many of the problems still facing us now could have been largely resolved. On August 5, 1959, *The Baltimore Sun* called attention to the Baltimore Planning Commission's delight at the suggestion that trees be planted in downtown Baltimore. The *Sun* also observed that, instead of planting trees, the Planning Commission recommended that "detailed plans and cost estimates" be drawn up by the Urban Renewal and Housing Agency, to be followed by contract negotiations relative to the work. According to the *Sun,* the city had trees available in its nursery and also had such other facilities as were needed to go ahead and plant trees in downtown Baltimore. With perhaps greater validity than charitableness, the *Sun* also said:

> . . . A small tree planted now will have reached imposing dimensions in the time that it otherwise would take to hire experts, hold conferences and finally reach agreement on what kind of trees should be planted where.

Former U. S. Housing Administrator Norman P. Mason made much the same type of charge in 1959. He asserted that: "In some areas, the planners seem to like to keep on planning and so rebuilding gets delayed." Mr. Mason also pointed up another factor which has contributed to high costs of urban renewal programs. He stated: "What too many local governments are grasp-

---

[38] *Ibid.*, pp. 20-36.

[39] See the Comptroller General of the United States, *A Report to the Congress of the United States: Review of Slum Clearance and Urban Renewal Program, Urban Renewal Administration, Housing and Home Finance Agency. As of June 1957; Review of Slum Clearance and Urban Renewal Activities in Puerto Rico, Urban Renewal Administration, Housing and Home Finance Agency, July 1958;* and *Audit of District of Columbia Redevelopment Land Agency, Fiscal Years 1957 and 1958, passim.*

ing for are more Federal grants, more and more of the United States taxpayers' dollars."[40] Instead of getting on with the job of urban renewal, municipal governments in many instances give the appearance of concentrating on efforts to secure federal monies. This of course delays the process of urban renewal and tends to force ultimate costs still higher.

We can summarize briefly some of the major factors which contribute to the high cost of urban renewal. The huge investments in our cities, when coupled with unavoidable attendant costs of deterioration, obsolescence, and resource-use changes, result in large costs for the urban renewal process. Simply adding up the individual costs involved leads to large aggregate cost figures. Previous neglect on the part of the cities confronts them with much accumulated decay in the form of blight, slums, and dilapidated and outmoded structures and facilities.

The vast scope of the federal urban renewal program which includes adding to the housing inventory, income redistribution via provision of subsidized housing for low-income occupants, slum clearance and rehabilitation, beautifying and face-lifting programs for the cities, revitalizing the cities—often apparently directing efforts against the tides of change—and the open-end character of the urban renewal program all contribute to high costs.

Notwithstanding the large cost estimates already cited, it is apropos to observe that undoubtedly they fall far short of the mark. Former Federal Urban Renewal Commissioner David A. Walker casts light on the reason for this.

> . . . At the beginning of planning, the cost of a new project is of no more than a guess. Federal and local records show that nine times out of ten, the guess has been wrong. As a result, the majority of capital grant reservations have to be increased when the firm estimates come in. . . .[41]

Costs also are raised because of upgrading based upon a desire to meet increased housing standards imposed by revised defini-

---

[40] Quoted in *The Sunday Star* (Washington), September 27, 1959.
[41] Quoted in HHFA-URA-No. 59-214, News Release of December 9, 1959, p. 1.

tions of standard quality housing. Costs are increased by the general imposition on consumers of housing standards above the minimum actually required for health and safety.

The bulldozer approach to urban renewal, which includes the razing of standard quality structures, adds to the costs of urban renewal programs. This mass clearance approach, in displacing many families, in turn contributes to slum formation in other parts of the cities, thus often nullifying the initial slum clearance and housing activities.

The practice of rewarding slum landlords, by paying inflated prices for slum properties based on the capitalized value of illegal earnings on those properties, again is a major factor in the high costs of urban renewal programs.

Finally, emphasis on planning urban renewal has tended to displace urban renewal itself. The federal urban renewal program involving as it does a minimum of two and generally four Federal agencies as well as local redevelopment authorities plus various commissions and departments of local government has become a complex and time-consuming operation. Many instances are reported wherein areas become ripe for urban renewal action through private initiative but lie dormant awaiting the outcome of the deliberations of government which may be years away. Delay in such cases unquestionably increases the final cost.

Emphasis on obtaining federal funds for local urban renewal activities has tended to replace the urban renewal activities themselves. Examples of this have appeared wherein the local public agency has gotten federal funds earmarked for one project and then moved on towards the same objective in a second, third, or fourth project meanwhile setting aside the first project because of lack of staff personnel to execute it.

FEDERAL VS. MUNICIPAL FINANCING

As noted earlier in the discussion of the legislative history of the federal urban renewal program, the existence of the federal program has been advocated partly on the assumption that state and municipal governments lack the financial resources to cope with "any substantial proportion" of the problem. There is considerable controversy about the accuracy of this view. There also is considerable doubt about both the meaning and the relevance of the assertion that the cities themselves are unable to finance urban renewal activities.

Nonetheless, alleged municipal incapacity to cope with municipal problems is widely asserted. Thus, the President's Advisory Committee on Government Housing Policies and Programs stated in 1953: "Most often the cities with the greatest slum problem have the least capacity to deal with it. Hence, the call for Federal aid."[42] Mayor Thomas D'Alesandro of Baltimore, in asking for federal funds, told a House committee: "Local governments simply do not have the resources available to them to assume a greater share of the financial burden for urban renewal."[43] Mayor Richard Daley of Chicago echoed this plea a few months later before a Senate subcommittee, asserting not only that cities were "willing" to finance urban renewal, but that increased federal requirements "for purposes of national and international security tend to limit the tax resources available to municipalities."[44] Mayor Daley subsequently pointed out: "It is the citizens of our metropolitan areas who contribute most heavily to the Federal and State Governments."[45] It appeared to be Mayor Daley's view that since so much of total federal tax revenues was derived from the cities it would be "equitable" to return a part of these monies to the cities as grants-in-aid for urban renewal programs. Mayor Daley also quoted the Chicago Association of Commerce and Industry as supporting essentially the same view.[46] Mayor Alvin G. Fields of East St. Louis, Illinois, in discussing federal aid stated:

---

[42] *Report of the President's Advisory Committee on Government Housing Policies and Programs, op. cit.*, p. 109.

[43] *Housing Act of 1959, Hearings, op. cit.*, p. 421.

[44] *President's Message Disapproving S. 57, Hearings*, U.S. Senate, Subcommittee of the Committee on Banking and Currency, 86th Congress, 1st Session, July 23-24, 27-31, 1959, p. 325.

[45] *Ibid.*

[46] *Ibid.*, pp. 324-25.

... [our] citizens are demanding more and more services, municipal costs are steadily increasing and the city's income simply does not increase at a rate that permits desirable and even necessary expenditures to be undertaken. Our resources are such that we cannot look at any other source to finance improvements.[47]

In a statement to the same subcommittee, Mr. Henry C. Beerits, President of the Philadelphia Housing Association, suggested that Philadelphia "might be entitled to perhaps $4\frac{1}{2}$ percent of the total that is available on a nationwide basis" and therefore they were advocating that Congress make an "appropriation" of $1 billion annually for urban renewal.[48] In this way, he said, Philadelphia could obtain the $45 million annually which they felt they needed.[49] Mr. Beerits asserted that "only the Federal Government has the resources to eliminate slums and blight."[50] This view that only the Federal Government can combat effectively municipal slums and blight has been widely expressed.

On the other hand, many persons are convinced that cities are perfectly capable of successfully combatting their slum and blight conditions. Some have noted that city failure to enforce adequate housing codes and city failure to perform normal city housekeeping services are the primary causes of slum conditions. Other witnesses representing the Eastwick Combined Committees of Philadelphia, told the same subcommittee (which had heard Mr. Beerits' testimony) that Philadelphia did not need the federal money demanded.[51] One witness, Miss Delores Rubillo stated, *inter alia:*

> The basis for the use of these Federal moneys is not need, but greed. Mr. Rafsky, city development coordinator, when faced with the fact that our community did not need this drastic redevelopment and that it was misuse of Government money to accomplish the project, stated that "if we don't get that money, someone else will." The general citizenry of the city are appalled at the attitude of our elected officials.[52]

---

[47] *Urban Renewal in Selected Cities, Hearings,* 1957, *op, cit.,* p. 91.
[48] *Ibid.,* pp. 877, 884.
[49] *Ibid.*
[50] *Ibid.,* p. 880.
[51] *Ibid.,* pp. 1140-45.
[52] *Ibid.,* p. 1145.

Miss Rubillo asserted that it was their position that the "willful demolition of good property with a resultant financial gain to private developers is not progress in a democratic nation."[53] She stated of the housing in the controversial Eastwick section which was scheduled for redevelopment by the city of Philadelphia:

> . . . They are not slums. We have some shacks. This is admitted. Any area has shacks. We have a lack of zoning enforcement. For the past 20 years there have been some houses standing which were condemned and never torn down.[54]

Much has been said to the effect that municipalities can finance their own renewal activities. Professor Monypenny, in an analysis of federal grants, made the following relevant observation:

> . . . Those cities whose fiscal difficulties are most prominently displayed house the greatest concentration of wealth.[55]

Professor Monypenny also discusses the political aspects of federal grants. Among other things, he makes the observation that federal grants-in-aid facilitate "the attainment of political objectives whose achievement was only possible if they were not too minutely specified."[56] He dismisses the contention that state and local governments cannot increase their revenues.[57]

Congressman Albert Rains, Chairman of the House Subcommittee on Housing, has attributed the apparent financing problems of localities not to an incapacity to raise revenues but to an unwillingness to do so. During the course of hearings on the 1959 Housing Act, he said:

---

[53] *Ibid.*, p. 1140.

[54] *Ibid.*, p. 1141. Another witness, Mr. Hillier, who appeared with Miss Rubillo, might have been influenced somewhat because of his personal objection to having to surrender his homestead. Among other things, Mr. Hillier said: ". . . I was told, that the home I live in, that I gave all my life struggle for, and desire to live in for the rest of my days, was too big for me. I was not entitled to a garden. I could live in two rooms." (p. 1143)

[55] Phillip Monypenny, "Federal Grants-in-Aid to State Governments; A Political Analysis," *National Tax Journal*, March 1960, p. 12.

[56] *Ibid.*, pp. 13-16.

[57] *Ibid.*, *passim*, esp. p. 12.

The people at the local level, the county governments and the State governments, the legislatures, don't have the intestinal fortitude it takes to put on the taxes to get what it takes to do the job.[58]

Thus, the argument seems to be that it is politically expedient to induce the Federal Government to serve as tax collector and return part of the proceeds to the states, counties, and municipalities. This frees local officials of the onus of responsibility for taxation and at the same time permits them to receive credit from their constituents for having obtained federal funds.

In essence, the claims and counter claims are, on the one hand, that only the Federal Government has the resources to eliminate slums and blight, and on the other hand that cities can cope with their slum problems.

Cities are uniquely equipped to enforce proper housing codes within their borders. Adequate enforcement of proper housing codes is a condition precedent to, and the essential element of, any effective urban renewal program. As Mr. Carter McFarland, an official of the Federal Government's Housing and Home Finance Agency, has pointed out, "strict enforcement of housing and neighborhood standards is a vital, but much neglected, ingredient of a comprehensive program of urban renewal."[59] To assert that cities lack the resources to enforce effective housing codes, the *sine qua non* of an effective urban renewal program, seems to deny the evidence of experience. Cities are as able to enact and enforce housing codes as they are to enforce their traffic regulations and fire codes. Therefore, in so far as the basic ingredient of urban renewal is concerned, cities *do* seem to have the ability and resources to eliminate slums and blight.

Federal grants-in-aid did not begin to expand rapidly until the depression of the 1930's, and at that time their rapid expansion was based not on federal revenues but upon federal deficit financing. "By 1930 all Federal grants totalled slightly over $100 mil-

---

[58] *Housing Act of 1959, Hearings, op. cit.*, p. 441.

[59] M. Carter McFarland, "The Urban Crisis," *Social Order*, October 1960, p. 365.

lion, four-fifths of which was for road building."[60] In 1959, federal grants-in-aid were close to $4 billion, quite apart from some $2.7 billion from the Highway Trust Fund.[61] By 1960, total federal aid to state and local governments had risen to $7.4 billion.[62]

While federal grants-in-aid have grown enormously in recent years, programs *already* committed undoubtedly will cause a substantial increase in the size of federal grants to states and local governments in future years.

The Federal Government now gets about two-thirds of the tax dollars.[63] Even so, the Federal Government is operating under severe fiscal pressures. War or defense requirements cannot be put off. Foreign subsidy programs which are related to national security not only are not likely to be reduced but are apt to be increased. The rising costs of burgeoning domestic programs of all kinds also are putting increased demands upon federal revenues—revenues already limited or scarce relative to demands being placed upon them.

As Mayor Daley of Chicago, Mr. McFarland, and many others have noted, our cities generate most of our income and contain most of our wealth. The greater part of this wealth is in the form of residential structures and in utilities and facilities which serve or are related to them. Housing itself is the largest single item in the inventory of national wealth.[64] Not only is most of the Nation's wealth in the cities, but also most of our income arises there. Mr. McFarland attributes 90 percent of our national income to 168 metropolitan areas and also observes that they have about three-quarters of the Nation's manufacturing capacity.[65]

---

[60] Roger A. Freeman, *Financing the Public Schools*, Vol. II: *Taxes for the Schools* (Washington: The Institute for Social Science Research, 1960), pp. 160-61.

[61] Charles F. Conlon, "The States Face the Sixties," *1959 Proceedings of the Fifty-Second Annual Conference on Taxation* (Harrisburg, Pennsylvania: National Tax Association, 1960), p. 22.

[62] Freeman, *op. cit.*, p. 163.

[63] *Ibid.*, p. 129.

[64] Nash, *op. cit.*, p. x.

[65] McFarland, *op. cit.*, p. 360.

If the Federal Government finances urban renewal it must secure the revenues largely from the cities themselves via taxation of their residents. (The alternative is to finance by means of deficit financing.)

It is often asserted that the cities and states cannot increase their revenues because the Federal Government has pre-empted so much of the potential tax revenue with its progressive income tax. It is claimed that it is not feasible for states or municipalities to try to impose income taxes on top of the heavy federal taxes. The latter is partly true, although it is worth noting that since state income taxes are deductible under the federal income tax laws, this amounts to at least a partial drawback of the federal levy in favor of the states' levies. Also, Mr. Roger Freeman, in his study on school financing points out: "With but few exceptions, all income, wealth, and transactions can be tapped by state as well as Federal tax laws."[66] But Mr. Freeman, in summarizing his discussion of the ability of different levels of government to finance various programs, says that the capacity to finance them depends upon several factors, and states:

> . . . Leading among them probably is the willingness of the people to devote a larger or smaller share of their income to public purposes, which, in turn, may depend on the specific use to which the money is to be put.[67]

This seems to be the crux of the matter.

Although the Federal Government does rely heavily on the income tax, local governments have the vital property tax as an important source of revenue. And *both* localities and states may turn to sales and excise taxes to a far greater extent that they have.

To summarize, most of our income and wealth is in the metropolitan areas. Present and committed federal expenditures already overstrain the federal budget. Cities and states have the power to raise additional revenues. They can do so if they can secure public support. If the public will not support the proposed revenue-expenditure programs, there is doubt of the wisdom of achieving by indirection (collecting funds through the

---

[66] Freeman, *op. cit.*, p. 127.
[67] *Ibid.*, p. 158.

Federal Government and remitting a part of the revenues to state and local governments) what cannot be achieved directly.

But of over-riding concern with respect to urban renewal is the point made by the President's Committee in 1953, as well as by many others, that the failure of cities adequately to enforce effective local housing codes and the failure of cities to perform the normal municipal functions of "housekeeping" are the primary causes of blight and slums. There is reason to doubt that voters are willing to finance certain kinds of urban renewal programs. There is no reason to doubt that municipalities have the capacity to finance effective urban renewal activities which command the support of their electorates.

CHAPTER VII

Some Problems of Cities

CONSIDERATION of urban renewal is more meaningful if accompanied by a recognition of some of the problems with which cities are confronted. Cities, like other institutions, have a varied assortment of problems. In so far as stating the problems requires recognition of inadequacies of many cities, we can view such inadequacies as opportunities for potential constructive action. In many instances the statement of the problem serves to indicate needed corrective measures.

Performance of Municipal Functions

Undoubtedly, a most serious charge leveled against the cities is that they, in general, have failed rather badly in the performance of those duties and functions which are peculiarly municipal in nature. Performance failure in these areas by municipal governments gives rise to many of the commonly voiced complaints about cities. Specifically, it is commonly said that many cities are dirty, noisy, ugly, characterized by undue violence, subject to extreme automobile traffic congestion, and lacking in parks and open space.

One of the great advantages of the city is the anonymity of city life. But the same anonymity which may grant some relief from social pressures for conformity also relieves the city dweller from social pressures which may operate toward upholding higher standards of public conduct. Large population concentrations or aggregations tend to break down the sense of personal involvement in the community, contribute to a sense of non-responsibility, and reduce, or at least are accompanied by a reduction in, effective participation in local affairs. The high mobility of our population reinforces these influences and further weakens active participation in community activities, particularly in large cities. The high proportion of renters as opposed to homeowners in cities serves also, in many cases, to weaken voter responsibility because of the tendency of tenants *not* to relate city expenditures and property taxes to the amount of their rent. Instead, the common tendency is to attribute the amount ("always too high"!) of the rent to the greed of landlords even though the landlord functions to some extent as a sort of informal tax collector. Successful urbanization requires not only a high standard of individual behavior, but also depends upon effective municipal government. Large concentrations of human beings require, in the interests of safety and health, more rigorous sanitation standards, fire codes, policing, and so on, than is necessary to achieve comparable conditions in less densely populated areas.

The oft-cited criticisms of cities largely reflect dissatisfaction with what municipal governments have done with respect to self-government. Cities as a whole have been and are delinquent in executing those municipal functions so often called housekeeping functions. Inadequate street lighting contributes to city crime as does inadequate patrolling of city streets by local police. Poor provision for garbage collection blights many city neighborhoods as does failure to compel the use of properly covered garbage containers. Many cities have miles of alleys littered with refuse. Such conditions constitute a health menace directly as well as indirectly in supporting disease-carrying rodents. Streets and alleys which are not clean and well-maintained reflect, and contribute to, the blighting of a city neighborhood.

Air and water pollution may be of small consequence in sparsely settled regions, but urban areas which permit pollution of air and water are quite a different matter. Noise abatement laws in many instances are recognized more in their breach than in their enforcement. This is true in many small communities as well as in cities, but the cities' problems are magnified by the sheer numbers concentrated within their limits. However, complaining of congestion in cities is somewhat like complaining of cold in Antarctica; the city by its nature is a place of congestion. That cities lack enough parks and open space is a commonplace observation. Yet cities by their nature are not open-space areas. In many cities there are hundreds of lots which are vacant or which contain unsafe structures. Many lots have clouded titles or are tax-delinquent. Effective municipal action could clean up many such lots and make them available either for new construction or for other uses.

In any event, the above and similar criticisms of the cities have been widely made and widely discussed. Likewise, the "flight to the suburbs" probably is at least partly related to criticisms of the cities. But the flight to the suburbs is affected by other factors. The search for "gracious living in the suburbs" and a more desirable place for children have played their parts in attracting many city dwellers to suburban life. The desire for a piece of land, however small, and for home ownership appears to have had its influence too. The automobile (and in many instances decline of "rapid" transit systems) and the relative cheapness and ease of assembly of suburban land have promoted the growth of the suburbs. Changing shopping conditions and practices have influenced the population shift. In some cases the influx to the city of minority group migrants has speeded the flight to the suburbs.

Population Growth

A large share of the suburban expansion is attributable to population growth. In many instances city geographical boundaries cannot be readily, if at all, expanded. Hence, the population explosion and metropolitanization of the Nation tend to lead to rapid expansion of the fringe areas surrounding the cities. On the other hand, there are persuasive indications that the flight to the suburbs has the quality of a real "flight." The determined opposition to the cities' annexation of surrounding suburbs and the lack of support for proposals to create super-city governments or metropolitan area-wide governments suggest a flight from the city as a political unit rather than merely a geographical movement. The pronounced movement of the middle classes to the suburbs and to exurbia would seem to further corroborate this. While many interesting implications and inferences inhere in the flight theory, the effects on the central cities are substantial and indeed may be self-reinforcing (an outflow of the middle classes may stimulate a further middle class out-migration).

The ghetto-like concentration of minority racial groups in certain areas in many cities is largely the result of social and cultural forces over which the city as a political unit has very little power. City governments, nevertheless, consistently tend to ignore the enforcement of housing codes (occupancy, safety, sanitation) in such areas. Partially as a result, members of minority groups often pay exorbitant rents for low-quality housing, the housing available to them within the confines of the area within which they may live.[1] Enforcement of adequate housing laws could assure better housing in these kinds of situations and thus curtail much of the spread of slums. Of considerable interest in this connection is the statement by local businessmen that code enforcement in Charlotte, North Carolina, "has had the additional effect of proving that Negro families are able and willing to pay for better housing and better neighborhoods."[2] However it may be viewed, the laxness of cities in establishing and enforcing effective codes and their failure to perform adequately municipal housekeeping and governmental functions are prime causes of much of the slum difficulties besetting cities today.

Change is characteristic of modern economies. The role of cities appears to be changing, particularly the role of central cities of metropolitan areas.[3] There are some indications that cities are regarded less as places in which to work and live and more as simply places in which to work, drawing upon surrounding suburban areas for a labor force which commutes to the city by day. Some observers believe that if the migration of the middle classes from the central cities continues, central cities will have as residents mainly the lower classes and the upper classes. The apparently changing character and role of the central cities has induced some to speculate that central cities are declining or dying institutions. While it is evident that in many respects central cities are of less relative importance than they

---

[1] This is a common and widely observed phenomenon. See, for example, *The Exploding Metropolis, op. cit.,* p. 120.

[2] Nash, *op. cit.,* pp. 87-88.

[3] For a recent discussion of this, see Raymond Vernon, *The Changing Economic Functions of the Central City* (New York: Committee for Economic Development, 1959).

once were, it is rather early to hold the obsequies. It seems imperative, however, that cities, as a matter of self-interest as well as in the interests of society at large, conduct their affairs in such a way as to facilitate, rather than to impede, orderly change. This involves proper city housekeeping, effective code enforcement and city planning, adequate revenue and expenditure policies, and good government generally. Renewal of the cities, to the extent that renewal is advantageous to the public, in turn, will be facilitated and hastened.

Taxes and Revenues

Presently it seems fashionable to declaim at length about the revenue difficulties of the cities. Yet, as previously noted, most of the Nation's wealth is located in the cities and it is in the cities that most of the Nation's income is earned. And, additionally, it is worth noting that there have been great increases in local revenues in recent years. Local tax receipts have increased much more than have federal tax receipts since the cessation of the Korean War. Local tax receipts increased more than state tax receipts during this period, but even state tax receipts increased much more than did those of the Federal Government. Percentage increases in tax receipts from 1952 through 1960 were:[4]

Governmental units:	Percentage increase in tax receipts:
Local	90.1
State	78.8
Federal	38.0

These figures do not tell the whole story, of course (for example, they do not indicate the relative revenue changes of specific local governments), but they do cast meaningful light on the notion that local governments lack revenue sources and that the Federal Government has unlimited sources.

---

[4] *Facts and Figures on Government Finance*, (11th ed., 1960-1961; New York: Tax Foundataion, Inc., 1961), Table 8, p. 21. The 1960 revenue figures were estimated by the Tax Foundation.

Shifting the costs of government urban renewal programs to the Federal Government is a device by which it appears that many localities hope to obtain funds, ostensibly from someone else and hence ostensibly to the advantage of the locality. The vast amorphous Federal budget facilitates this belief or hope and, in turn, opposition to expenditures for marginal and sub-marginal purposes is weakened. Cities can tap the resources within their borders to finance urban renewal programs. States can tap the resources within their borders. The fundamental problem which faces these governmental units is that of securing public support for their programs. The more intimately related government revenue-expenditure proposals are, the more likely the public is to make decisions which closely reflect the public scale of value preferences. Generally, the public have shown a remarkable willingness to surrender their money to government. Current complaints by city (and other) governments that they have inadequate revenues and lack adequate sources of revenues in reality indicates a collective judgment on the part of the electorate as to the scope and amount of resources that should be devoted to public functions. The revenue problems of city and other governments are, in many instances, problems of excessive governmental expenditures.

City practices with respect to taxation and tax delinquent lands appear to be important contributing causes of city problems. A study made in Flint, Michigan, prior to World War II, indicated that city problems of excessive services costs (garbage collection, water, sewers, and police and fire protection) were related to indirect subsidies which the city provided sub-division developers and speculators.[5]

A closely related cause of city revenue problems is the tendency to over-tax good properties and to under-tax slum properties. Under-taxation of slum properties appears to derive from tax appraisals which are heavily weighted by consideration of the physical condition of structures on the land site. Frequently,

---

[5] Edmund N. Bacon, "A Diagnosis and Suggested Treatment of an Urban Community's Land Problem," *The Journal of Land and Public Utility Economics*, February 1940, *passim*.

it has been pointed out that dilapidated slum structures are located on what is asserted to be very valuable land. And earnings or the rates of return on slum properties often are very high. When slum properties are under-taxed, the local taxing unit in effect is indirectly penalizing owners who maintain properties in good condition and at the same time subsidizing the slum owners. Also, in many cases, high tax delinquency on slum properties further reduces potential revenue. Slum ownership is further encouraged by lax code enforcement which of itself contributes greatly to the existence of slums. Beyond this, under-taxation of slum properties also may encourage speculation in such properties by minimizing the tax costs of ownership, costs which are transferred to other property owners. Some observers have been so distressed by this phenomenon that they have advocated heavy land or situs taxation both to prevent slums and to avoid land speculation.[6] These proposals usually are related also to their advocates' desire to cause land to be used in ways which accord with their (the advocates) personal value judgments.[7] It is not necessary to resort to Georgian single-tax-on-land proposals in order to eliminate unfair tax advantages which may be enjoyed by the owners of slum properties. Much of the desirability and opportunity for speculative profits can be removed from slum and substandard housing by strict enforcement of adequate housing codes.

Closely related to the tendency to under-tax slum properties is the widespread dereliction in clearing clouded titles on vacant lots and municipal failure to turn to the city's advantage tax delinquent properties. Tax delinquent properties and those with clouded titles might well be utilized by the municipality for various purposes or made available, at market prices, for new construction.

---

[6] See, for example, H. Bronson Cowan, *Municipal Improvement and Finance* (New York: Harper & Brothers, 1958), *passim*. (This is a report prepared for the International Research Committee on Real Estate Taxation.) Also see *House & Home*, August 1960, *passim*, but esp. pp. 123-24, 131-43.

[7] *Ibid.*

Restrictions on Production

Excessively high building and construction costs in some cities have contributed to the cities' problems by discouraging new construction and thus impeding renewal. Outmoded building codes frequently play a vital part in limiting new construction in many major cities. Thus, for example, the prefabricated steel Lustron house (now defunct) could not be erected in some of our major cities because its steel construction did not meet city fire code requirements of plaster wall construction. Also, the view is widely held that restrictions on the introduction of labor-saving devices under labor union contracts, union wage scales, and union influence over local building codes operate to raise costs and thus to curtail the volume of construction. Indirect restrictions (via the price mechanism) are quite as restrictive as direct constraint. The opportunities for encouraging construction by adopting modern, reasonable building codes and by eliminating restraints of trade are substantial in the very large cities, the areas in which such restraints are most effectively imposed at present.

Governmental Action

Governmental action has contributed to, and magnified, the problems of cities in many instances. Rent controls during and after World War II stimulated illegal conversions and in effect put a premium on permitting the physical deterioration of rental properties.[8] Rent controls not only contributed to a mis-allocation of resources but they also undoubtedly exercised negative effects on rental housing construction. New York City, which still imposes rent controls (although not on new construction), has a distorted, segmented into free and controlled, rental housing market. The fact that new construction is not controlled seems rather good evidence of some of the effects of rent control upon the housing supply.

---

[8] The merits or necessity for rent controls in time of war or national emergency are not argued here. Rather, only their resulting effects upon housing are considered.

Federal Government intervention in the housing market doubtless has at least contributed to the movement to the suburbs and to the problems of the central cities. Louis Winnick, in the Preface to his detailed study of the rental housing market, in discussing the impact of federal intervention in this area says:

> . . . It is, by now, beyond argument that the net effect of government entry into the housing market over the past two decades has been a contraction in the volume of rental building through policies calculated to benefit the home buyer and home builder and policies, less calculated, to penalize the equity investor in rental housing.[9]

The "less calculated" results to which Mr. Winnick refers are in many respects worse than those specifically intended because they are unintended or unforeseen consequences which in turn often generate demands for further intervention to offset them. Further government intervention may then create in turn additional unforeseen distortions and the problem-creating process resultant from governmental intervention becomes more pronounced.

Government urban renewal programs themselves often are examples of this kind of intervention. Not only are urban renewal programs, which ignore the question of returns relative to outlays, being planned and executed but also they are setting in motion whole series of corollary effects, many of which unquestionably will be disadvantageous to the public welfare. The choice of the example of federal subsidies to farmers, cited by local politicians to bolster their demands for federal subsidies for urban renewal programs, is hardly reassuring. One of the primary weaknesses of the present federal urban renewal program is that the subsidy destroys, or rather, perverts, the process of equating marginal returns. As a result, resource allocative decisions are often misguided.

One interesting proposal for overcoming some of these objections has been advanced by Mr. Otto Davis. Mr. Davis has suggested that cities themselves might undertake to act as "rational

---

[9] Louis Winnick, *Rental Housing: Opportunities For Private Investment* (New York: McGraw-Hill Book Co., 1958), p. xx. See also the overall import of his textual discussion, *passim.*

entrepreneurs."[10] The city could decide upon the area to be redeveloped, raise money through bond sales, secure property through condemnation, demolish inadequate structures, and sell the land.[11] Decisions could be made on the basis of the anticipated profitability to the city of the action, including receipts derived from land sales and the discounted present value of the estimated net addition to property tax revenues. Where cities lack the legal powers to carry through such a program, state enabling legislation might clear the way. Mr. Davis' proposal seems to base urban renewal programs on rational plans and to subject any urban renewal activity to the skeptical scrutiny of potential investors.

Land Assembly

In virtually every discussion of urban renewal and redevelopment, the problem of difficulty of land assembly is raised. Generally it is posed as a well-nigh insuperable problem barring a program of government condemnation and subsidization for acquisition and clearance. It is frequently pointed out that a developer often can secure a hundred-acre or even a thousand-acre tract outside the city from a few owners or sometimes a single owner with relative ease. To acquire a comparable tract within the city may require negotiations with dozens of owners, some of whom may refuse, for speculative or other reasons, to sell properties which may be vital to the project which is being considered. There may be clouded titles on some lots, some owners may be hard to locate, perhaps living in remote parts of the world, and so on. These and other difficulties may make the assembly of a suitable tract of land, even in a slum area, prohibitively costly and time consuming.

That the problems of land assembly in the city are real and may hinder renewal is widely accepted. However, a number

---

[10] Otto A. Davis, "A Pure Theory of Urban Renewal," *Land Economics*, May 1960, esp. pp. 224-26.

[11] The Indianapolis, Indiana, program discussed earlier is in many respects similar to Mr. Davis' proposal.

of states have recently adopted "quick taking" laws to expedite land assembly.

> . . . Upon filing a declaration of taking (containing a description of the land, the interest taken, the authority under which taken, and the public use involved) and the deposit of an estimate of the just compensation with the court, title immediately vests in the condemnor, and the right to just compensation vests in the former owner. . . . Pending a later judicial determination of the just compensation, [and the owners entitled thereto] the state is free to use the condemned property.[12]

Also dereliction on the part of many cities in the performance of certain municipal governmental functions is a contributing cause to these difficulties of land assembly. These derelictions already have been developed in the preceding discussions of the problems of cities, but their specific relevance to the difficulties encountered in assembling suitable tracts of land for redevelopment purposes in the cities should be examined.

The failure to squeeze abnormal profits out of ownership of slum properties is an important factor in making ownership of these properties attractive. That slum ownership is a rewarding investment in many instances is evident partly by the fact that landlords do not disinvest from slum holdings but more so by the continued flow of investment funds into such properties. The high returns often possible in slum ownership place a premium on slum investments and materially raise the capitalized values of slum properties, thus serving as a deterrent to their sale except at markedly inflated prices. This in turn raises the costs of any proposed redevelopment program dependent upon acquisition of slum properties. Strict minimal code enforcement relative to health, safety, and housing standards would contribute much to eliminating the excessive returns earned on slum properties and thus would facilitate renewal or redevelopment.

Closely allied to the foregoing is the tendency to under-tax slum properties. Under-taxation of slum properties amounts to an indirect subsidy granted by the city government and hence also impedes land assembly and redevelopment since the indirect

---

[12] Haar, *op. cit.*, p. 497.

subsidy in the form of under-taxation increases the profitability of slum properties. Inadequate code enforcement and under-taxation make speculation in slum properties relatively more attractive than it otherwise would be and by encouraging speculative hold-outs for higher prices raise the costs of land acquisition for redevelopment.

The failure to clear clouded land titles also interferes with land assembly, making it a more costly process than it otherwise would be, and hence impeding possible redevelopment activities by potential investors. This is not to imply that there would be no problems of land assembly if the city vigorously pursued the indicated actions. However, adequate code enforcement, proper taxation of slum properties, and clearing of clouded titles all would be conducive to redevelopment of the city not only in the sense of public acquisition of properties for demolition, but in the broader urban renewal sense of encouraging or forcing private property owners to maintain their properties more adequately, to use them so as not to contribute to the creation of slums, and to facilitate changes in land use.

CHAPTER VIII

A Constructive Program
For Urban Renewal

THE URBAN RENEWAL problem in the broad sense has been with us for decades and will remain in the future. It is not something that suddenly descended upon us and once cleared up (if possible?) can be considered over with.

The essence of the problem can easily be seen if we were to imagine a wholly new city constructed in accord with the best plans. Although the entire city and its supporting facilities were completely new, problems of renewal would appear within a few years. Physical depreciation would take its toll. Obsolescence would affect parts of the city increasingly as a result of growth and technological development. These, and other factors, such as changes in costs and in consumer preferences, would give rise to a need for adjustments in the use of land as well as of various structures and supporting facilities. Thus, within the short time of a few years, the hypothetical new city would be confronted with some of the same kinds of renewal problems which cities face today. The difference between the hypothetical new city and our real cities is simply that real cities typically are not constructed all at one time but tend to develop over a period of time.

There is nothing mysterious about these renewal problems. They are as old as our earliest cities and they will be with us as long as there are urban concentrations. Urban renewal by its nature is a continuing process of repair, removal, replacement, and changing usage. During Senate hearings in 1959, Mr. John R. Searles, Jr., then President of the National Association of Housing and Redevelopment Officials and Executive Director of the District of Columbia Redevelopment Land Agency, recognized this continuing nature of urban renewal. While Mr. Searles was requesting more funds for the federal programs and believed that approximately $13 billion would be needed during the next

10 years for these programs, he stated that "we know there has got to be some continuing level [of federal aid] that will probably go on forever."[1] Thus, he responded to a question relative to the length of time it would take to "complete the job." Urban renewal in fact will take "forever," because by its nature it cannot be "completed" and then set aside. This is not to say, of course, that the *federal* grant-in-aid urban renewal program need go on forever.

During the course of the preceding discussion a variety of factors have been noted which contribute to the problems confronting our cities. We have analyzed our housing supply; we have described local, state, and federal action aimed at improving its quality; we have summarized the development of supporting legislation and have compared the opinions of recognized authorities regarding its constitutionality; and finally we have reviewed results achieved under the various programs.

We have seen the great reliance which is being placed on the federal urban renewal program, but we have also seen the minuscule results, the enormous cost in federal and local grants, and above all the snail's pace at which the whole process moves. Apparent remedies include the elimination of red tape in processing, and provision of some means of faster acquisition, assembly and disposition of redevelopment land by local public agencies. The former could be accomplished in large measure by the removal of the federal agencies' (URA, HHFA, PHA, and FNMA), participation. This would also mean the elimination of federal subsidy. However, there seems good ground to argue that abandonment of federal aid along with the related complicated procedures might be a net benefit. On the other hand, it is a near certainty that availability of larger grants will have little effect on the pace of a program which in ten years has consistently lagged behind congressional authorization of money for the program.

The matter of faster land assembly and disposition is related to exercise of the right of eminent domain under due process

---

[1] *Housing Act of 1959, Hearings, op. cit.,* pp. 569-70.

of law. Yet, we have seen in the previous analysis how the power to take private property for public use has been stretched to great lengths already. It seems reasonable to conclude then that whether federal participation is continued or discontinued the present type of urban renewal program must hereafter be cast in a minor role in the war against slums and that other machinery must be geared to greater productivity.

Yet there is reason for optimism about the opportunities and practicable possibilities for further improvement in the quality of our cities. There has been a remarkable increase in the housing inventory relative to population growth during the past two decades. In addition to the quantitative growth in the housing inventory, there also has been a striking improvement in the quality of the housing inventory.

The 1950 Census of Housing showed 17,881,000 substandard housing units. In 1956 this had declined to 14,589,000 and by 1960, to 10,952,000.[2] Recognizing that the increase in housing supply during this period was somewhat less than the volume of new construction, it must be concluded that part of the decline in substandard houses has been achieved by the natural process of elimination. However, it is safe to say that a large part of the improvement was the result of rapidly increasing annual expenditures of private funds on repair, improvement, renovation, and modernization. Such expenditures are estimated by the Home Improvement Council to have risen from an estimated $10-$12 billion in 1955 to $18-$20 billion in 1960.[3] Further improvement is to be expected as market forces continue to operate to raise the standards of housing.

The following lines of action seem to be basic to improving the quality of our cities and to facilitating the urban renewal process. None of these will compel land resources to be used for a given

---

[2] Including dilapidated units and those lacking one or more of the following facilities: private toilet or bath, or hot or cold running water. Also includes 1,481,000 in 1950 and 1,961,000 units in 1956 on which condition was not reported.

[3] See "The Fix-Up Market," *Barron's*, May 22, 1961, p. 11.

specific purpose. However, if carried out, they will facilitate the process of urban renewal where renewal is economically and socially advantageous, and also will contribute to the vitality and quality of our cities. This is not to suggest that employing these measures would solve all city problems or eliminate all unsightly areas or even all slums. By whatever standards we employ there will always be some units which are categorized as the lowest quality within the universe. Hence, even if quality of housing and cities generally were doubled, some units and resources would be at the bottom level of quality.

None of these proposals is a cure-all of itself. Action is needed with respect to all of them. Nor are they dramatic. Unfortunately, perhaps, it seems that practical urban renewal measures are apt to be pedestrian rather than theatrical. These lines of action nevertheless provide ample challenges to keep those interested in urban renewal activities productively engaged during the foreseeable future.

Improvement of Municipal "Housekeeping" Services

In virtually all cities the possibilities for improving the quality of municipal services are substantial.

In most cities there is a noticeable tendency to provide satisfactory maintenance of public facilities in certain select areas, while providing less satisfactory maintenance in other large areas of the city. Streets, alleys, and sidewalks should be maintained in clean and good condition throughout the city. Regular and frequent collections of refuse and garbage is most necessary to this.

As areas of the city age, and more particularly where occupancy changes to a lower income group, cities often tend to reduce their services and become lax in the enforcement of municipal regulations. Thus, housing structures in older residential areas are converted into smaller units, occupancy codes may be disregarded, excessive crowding occurs, and cities tend to permit such areas to become slums. If slum conditions are to be minimized, municipal services and enforcement of minimal standards of safety and health must be fully maintained in aging and changing neighborhoods. Areas which are wearing out must be maintained in safe and healthful conditions even though they are of declining value and prestige.

Property Taxes

Revision of real property tax assessments so as to achieve a better balance between land or site taxation and taxation of improvements or structures has great merit and appears to be attracting increasing attention. Land now carries a smaller share of the realty tax load than it has in the past. *House & Home* points out that today land carries but one-third of the realty tax, whereas 50 years ago it carried two-thirds.[4] *House & Home* also stresses the dangers of undue land speculation and urges that higher land taxes might contribute to reducing such excessive speculation.[5] It would be possible in many jurisdictions to raise taxes on land relative to structures so that taxes would be more in line with the location value of the land and the municipal facilities made available to the site.

In any event, the problem of slums may be mitigated by imposing a more realistic tax load on slum properties. Present taxation practices frequently in effect subsidize slum properties. Generally, taxes on slum properties are quite low, even though it may be acknowledged that the site of a slum structure is very valuable and/or that earnings from a slum structure are relatively high. Higher taxation on substandard and slum properties, taxation more in line with earnings and/or site values, would tend to bring down the profits of slum ownership, thus establishing conditions conducive to demolition of slum structures and to the normal renewal of slum areas as well as aiding in increasing revenues.

---

[4] *House & Home*, August 1960, p. 139.

[5] *Ibid.*, esp. pp. 134-39. Although *House & Home* is extremely critical of land speculation, a footnote on page 136 indirectly or implicitly acknowledges that land speculation involves risk assumption as does other speculation and ownership.

Clearance of Lot Titles and Tax Delinquencies

Obscure or confused titles are serious impediments to land acquisition and new building. In some instances the existence of clouded titles may deter the execution of a substantial redevelopment project. Legal action by the cities, facilitated where necessary by state legislation, to expedite the clearance of property titles could help overcome the spotty development often seen within cities and provide a sounder basis for municipal revenues.

Closely allied is the problem of tax-delinquent properties. In some jurisdictions a property owner may fail to meet his realty taxes for a number of years, lose the property to the city, and then repurchase it under conditions which amount to a wiping out of his delinquent taxes.[6] Thus the city subsidizes speculation, loses tax revenues, and encourages the holding of vacant properties (or, discourages their sale for new buildings). Effective property tax collection procedures would contribute to more efficient use of land, more city revenues, and new construction, thus aiding urban renewal.

Code Enforcement

Code enforcement is not a cure-all for bad housing and slum conditions in our cities, but it is one of the most important weapons which can be employed in combating slums.

Former President Herbert Hoover wrote:

> I may add an observation on slum clearance. There is scarcely a city where, if the health and building laws were adequately enforced, a large part of the slums would not be empty of tenants. There is no provision in morals or freedom or the Constitution that building owners be allowed to collect income from the pollution of public health and morals in the name of private property.[7]

---

[6] See Bacon, *op. cit.*, p. 85, for a detailed example of this process.

[7] Herbert Hoover, *The Memoirs of Herbert Hoover, The Cabinet and the Presidency, 1920-1933* (New York: The Macmillan Company, © 1952), p. 258. Quotation used by permission of the Macmillan Company.

The Federal Urban Renewal Administration has emphasized the importance of conserving those assets which cities now have, rather than merely encouraging the wholesale destruction and rebuilding of our cities. Thus, in a recent pamphlet entitled "Home Improvement . . . Lessons from Experience," the Urban Renewal Administration said:

> . . . Existing dwellings constitute the greatest housing resource at our disposal.
>
> ❀   ❀   ❀
>
> . . . Our cities cannot be renewed nor blight eliminated and potential blight arrested by clearance and redevelopment alone. Only by utilizing conservation and rehabilitation as well as clearance can a successful attack on urban decay be accomplished.[8]

Zoning, building, and housing codes are the basic tools for dealing with urban renewal problems. Zoning ordinances are concerned with use compatibility of land and structures. Building codes are concerned with construction, primarily to assure safe structures. Increasingly, emphasis is being given to substituting performance requirements for specific structural material requirements in building codes. Performance requirements allow greater flexibility and in many instances permit lower construction costs. Housing codes essentially are concerned with minimal housing conditions and emphasize the assurance of minimum sanitation and health conditions in housing. Housing codes may establish minimum requirements as to shelter quality of the dwelling, plumbing, and occupancy. Effective enforcement of adequate zoning, building and housing codes, offers enormous possibilities in protecting cities from blight and slum formation and in promoting urban renewal.

New York State, in cooperation with the Housing and Home Finance Agency recently issued a three-volume series of pamphlets under the general series title of *Housing Codes, The Key*

---

[8] Bulletin 2, Urban Renewal Service (Washington: Housing and Home Finance Agency, Urban Renewal Administration, October 1960), p. 1.

to *Housing Conservation.*[9] Volume I gives a "Background of Code Enforcement"; Volume 2 suggests a "Model Housing Code"; and Volume 3 is an "Administrative Guide" to code enforcement programs. The literature on housing problems contains many varied considerations and analyses of different aspects of code enforcement. Nevertheless, it is almost universally agreed that city codes tend to be inadequate both in content and in enforcement.

Some housing and urban renewal officials dismiss code enforcement as being of relatively little value, citing the difficulties of securing compliance, pointing out that codes do not build housing units, and asserting that code enforcement may interfere with long-range planning. During the last session of Congress an unsuccessful effort was made to make cities ineligible for federal renewal or public housing grants until they have a minimum housing code and a record of satisfactory enforcement for at least one year.[10]

Code enforcement is difficult, as is the enforcement of any legislation. Complete compliance probably never is secured with any legislation, but general compliance with reasonable legislative measures is common. We do not fail to enforce traffic regulations simply because universal compliance cannot be secured at all times.

Minimal housing code requirements will not build housing units but enactment and enforcement of up-to-date housing codes can assure the safe and healthful maintenance and operation of existing occupied structures.

It is said (and is true) that requiring compliance with housing codes could raise costs subsequently of planned government projects necessitating the acquisition of the properties if additional investments in structures are passed on to government in condemnation proceedings. Yet the present system of permitting slums has led to enormously inflated costs of acquiring slum properties. Requiring compliance with reasonable housing code standards could by reducing the profits in slum properties, reduce their

---

[9] (New York: State of New York, Division of Housing, 1960), three volumes.

[10] *Congressional Record,* June 22, 1961, pp. 10330-32.

values and acquisition costs.[11] In fact, it could be argued that this should be a prerequisite step to acquisition.

Long-range planning of land uses is possible whether codes are enforced or not. In any event, technological changes and possible land-use changes cannot be predicted with any certainty. Failure to enforce codes on the grounds that long-range plans may require demolition of the structures concerned seems unrealistic. Many plans are never executed and only a small fraction of a city's structures will be subject to demolition because of needed government projects. Finally, there is little logic in permitting the operation of structures which endanger public health or safety merely on the grounds that their ultimate demolition is being planned. (We would consider it irresponsible to permit the operation of defective motor vehicles which endangered public safety on the grounds that their owners were considering junking them and replacing them with new machines at some time in the future. Housing which endangers public health or safety is likewise a menace, even though less dramatic.)

Effective enforcement of reasonable housing standards would require only that housing units be maintained in healthful and safe condition and in conformity with occupancy standards. It is not suggested that housing codes be used as a cloak to permit the destruction (value or physical) of housing structures merely because they do not meet someone's standards of beauty or architectural design.[12]

Consider the advantages of housing code enforcement. Code enforcement, though never fully applied, has resulted in sub-

---

[11] A curious aspect of the "cost" objection to code enforcement is that often those who so object see little objection to purchasing slum properties at enormous cost to the Government and with great gain to the owners of slum properties in many instances.

[12] Another objection that is sometimes raised with respect to more strict code enforcement has to do with the financial inability of some owner-occupants of substandard housing to comply with housing code requirements. This is generally a problem in a few scattered cases. Some cities have developed specialized loan funds (Fight Blight Funds) to handle this problem. There are many other ways of dealing with it also.

stantial improvements in the quality of substandard housing (as in the City of Charlotte, North Carolina). Consistent housing code enforcement will contribute to more realistic depreciation allowances for aging properties, including the discounting of future expectations in line with the useful life of the structure. This in turn will contribute to lower values for slum properties, thus encouraging the demolition of low-earning structures. Values and offering prices for slum properties would fall if owners' and prospective buyers' future expectations were affected by knowledge of enforced repair, maintenance, and eventual demolition costs which would be borne by them. The great profitability of slum ownership is one of the severest impediments to the smooth functioning of the process of urban renewal. It hinders the removal of worn-out parts of the housing inventory. Code enforcement will hasten the process of vacating and demolishing inadequate structures. Each such cleared site constitutes an improvement per se and is a step towards subsequent rebuilding or other reuse.

In some crowded areas of the city, lots which have reverted to city ownership might be set aside as playground areas. This would help overcome undue population density in such areas and provide a bit more open space within the confines of the city. Over the long run, the desideratum would be maintenance of all areas of the city in at least a safe and healthful condition, vacating and demolishing outworn structures, with new construction taking place in the midst of older, well-maintained buildings.

Housing demand has been leveling off as war-postponed and other demand has been largely satisfied. There is less doubling of families in housing units and in many areas the vacancy rates are higher than they have been for some years.[13] The decade of the 1960's promises to be an excellent time in which to inaugurate systematic housing code enforcement in the Nation's metropolitan areas.

Code enforcement, tax reform, and title clearance could contribute greatly to reducing the presently difficult problem of

---

[13] See U.S. Bureau of the Census, *Current Housing Reports, Housing Vacancies*, Series H-111, No. 23, January 1961.

assembling within the city parcels of land large enough to be useful for redevelopment projects.

Urban Renewal

The process of urban renewal as we have come to know it under the "project type" program probably should be continued locally as an important but minor part of the much broader under- *why?* taking of conserving and upgrading the entire inventory of housing. It should ideally operate free from stifling dependency upon federal grants, (possibly in somewhat the manner of the Indianapolis program). Its objective could be limited to planning and executing special purpose projects which are beyond the scope of the improved housekeeping and enforcement functions previously mentioned. It should operate under close scrutiny of the elected representatives of the locality. If these conditions are maintained the local urban renewal program can be expected to contribute to the welfare, quality, and utility of the city and at the same time minimize the impact of renewal activities upon the basic rights of individual property owners.

The lines of action set forth above in brief form offer ample opportunities for intensive efforts by city officials and laymen alike and should not involve vast governmental expenditures. The measures are aimed at reducing slum conditions, at conserving the vast real property within our cities, and at providing conditions conducive to land-use changes. They are not advanced as final "solutions" or as suggesting that other measures may not be required as well, although these measures should be given priority. They will not guarantee the prosperous revival of an area which is in decline. Consequently some will not find these proposals as satisfactory as a federal subsidy program. However, the federal program does not seem necessary to meet the reasonable requirements of urban renewal.

Since the urban renewal process is a continuous one, clearing present pockets of substandard and slum housing in some of our cities in the long view is somewhat beside the point. Nor is it very likely that a federal grant-in-aid program that helps get rid

[125]

of some worn-out parts of a city on a project-by-project basis will have much lasting, overall effect unless within the community, measures are instituted for assuring better use of urban resources on a continuous, long-range basis. If this latter is accomplished the need for the former is largely removed or at least greatly lessened. Good housing, clean cities, and urban renewal are basically local functions and problems—the federal program recognizes this and intends, through the "workable program" concept, to use the federal grant as a carrot to induce the locality involved to undertake such measures. Unless local interest is desirous of having a clean town or city, free of substandard housing, such will not occur—no matter how much federal money is obtained. Few, if any, American cities do such a job well—some do very little. But the interest in urban renewal in recent years may be the beginning of an awareness that we must cultivate better urban manners and no longer allow property owners the luxury of creating slums with their properties.

Table of Cases

Index

Occupied Dwelling Units by Location, Tenure, and Condition 1956, Table, 12

Percentage Increases in Population and Housing, SMA's, Table, 16

relocation housing, 34-35, 40

quality, 9, 11

Housing Units by Condition 1950, 1956 and 1960, Table, 10

Housing Act of 1949, 30-37
H.H.F.A. hypothetical project, 32-34

Housing Act of 1954, 37-41

Housing Act of 1959, 41-42

Housing Act of 1961, 42-43, 70

Housing and Home Finance Agency
appropriation bill of 1954, 38
associated agencies, chart, 45
Housing Act of 1949, 31
Housing Act of 1954, 37-39
role in urban renewal, 31, 52
"workable program," 52

Indianapolis, Ind., 72, 112n.

Los Angeles, Calif., 71-72

Louisville, Ky., 29, 47-49

Mason, Norman P., 79, 85, 93

Maywood, Ill., 88

McCollum, John P., 84

McFarland, Carter, 99, 100

Monypenny, Phillip, 98

Nash, William W., 71n.

National Industrial Recovery Act of 1933, 28-29

New York
Housing code, 26-27
New York City, 87-88, 110

Nilsson, George W., 63-64

"Nuisance Doctrine," 25-26

Oklahoma, 55

Oklahoma City, 50

Philadelphia, Pa., 26, 97

Pitt, William, 46

Pittsburgh, Pa., 72

"Police Powers," 7, 25-26

Population
central cities, 15-16, 24
increases, 13
suburban, 15-16, 24
urban metro. areas, 1, 15-16

President's Advisory Committee on Government Housing Policies and Programs, 27, 37, 68, 69, 77, 86-87, 96, 102

Public Housing Administration
H.H.F.A., relationship to, chart, 45
low-rent housing, 53
role in urban renewal, 53

Rains, Albert, 98

Reconstruction Finance Corp., 29

Richberg, Donald, 54

Rubillo, Delores, 97-98

St. Louis, Mo., 71

San Francisco, Calif., 89-90

Searles, John R., Jr., 115-116

Steiner, Richard L., 79

Slums
anti-social behavior, 23
causes, 86
character, 23
development, 2, 37
federal seizure of property, 29
Housing Act of 1949, 30-31

Standard Metropolitan Areas
defined, 15
housing changes, 11, 15, 16, 17
population changes, 15-16

Taxes, 107-109, 119

Thomas, Albert, 79

Turchon, Peter, 73

U. S. Housing Act of 1937, 29-30

U. S. Housing Authority, 30

Urban Renewal Administration
H.H.F.A., relationship to, chart, 45
role in urban renewal program, 51, 65